# Self Regulation for Teens

# Teens

An 8 Step Survival Guide for the Teenage Brain to Overcome Stress, Manage Emotions, Achieve Goals, and Thrive for Life.

Brenda Emerson

acknowledge that the author is not engaging in the rendering of legal, financial, medical or professional advice. The content within this book has been derived from various sources. Please consult a licensed professional before attempting any techniques outlined in this book.

By reading this document, the reader agrees that under no circumstances is the author responsible for any losses, direct or indirect, which are incurred as a result of the use of information contained within this document, including, but not limited to, — errors, omissions, or inaccuracies.

# Table of Contents

# Introduction

I felt like I was living in a world made entirely of concrete and brick, and it was suffocating me. I didn't understand where I'd gone wrong. When I was younger, my parents had always said they loved me. They'd take me to nice restaurants and would buy me toys when I was young, and I had a lot of friends. But when I got older, our relationship drifted apart and I started having trouble with achieving good grades. I developed anger issues and I was so lonely. I didn't feel like talking to someone about it, because I was afraid they'd think I was crazy. I felt like a failure all the time. Everything seemed so overwhelming, and nothing made sense anymore. I remember how one day in class, the teacher asked us all to write about our dreams for the future. The teacher looked at each one of us as we wrote down what we wanted to do with our lives—but when it came time for my turn, I just sat there blankly with my pen in my hand. That made me feel even worse about myself and what kind of person everyone thought I was becoming because everyone else seemed happier than ever before except for me who was still sad all the time. I'd also been having trouble sleeping. Something was off, some kind of feeling that I couldn't quite name. All I know is that it felt like something needed to change. I was depressed and hopeless. But then, I found a new way of dealing with the situation. It started when I realized that the reason why I was so down was because of my own negative thoughts about myself. My mind would always think that things were not good enough, and I would start believing those thoughts too. So, I decided to do something about it. To change my mind from being a victim of my own thinking, and think more positively instead! The first step that I took was to look at all the good things in life: the sun coming out after a storm; the beautiful sunset that you see in pictures; the smell of freshly baked cookies. With these positive images in front of me every day, it became easier and easier for me to think positively about myself and my mood improved as well! This realization helped me build my therapeutic techniques, which are the crux of this book.

And when I became a parent myself, these techniques helped me understand myself and my children in their emotional healing journey. I wanted to write this book for all the teenagers who are somehow stuck and would like to develop their skills in overcoming their emotional distress and anxiety. In this book, I'll introduce you to 8 simple steps to managing emotions for young adults and teenagers. These are practical solutions that will shift your negative mindset and help you gain self-confidence to live a happier life, and help you understand the root causes of your emotional outbursts to nip the ailment in its bud. They'll help you develop self-control and patience by teaching you how to focus on the present moment to make better decisions about how to act in the future. The techniques outlined in this book are easy to implement, and they work!

The most important step in learning how to manage your emotions is admitting that there's a problem. I understand you might feel alone right now, but you aren't, and it takes a village to raise a child! It's hard in the world today when so many people are lonely and sad, and feel they don't have the tools to deal with these emotions. I know this because I've seen it happen again and again in my own family. "I've been there." Frankly enough, that's the first thing I tell people who come to me for help because I know what it's like to be in a place where you feel like things are out of control. You want to do the right thing, but the only way to do that is to get in touch with someone who knows how to help you, and that's exactly what this book is for. It's designed to be a safe space where readers can understand their emotional ties and work on them together. It's also designed to be a resource they can use on their own time if they need it, so they can read and learn from other people who have been through similar things or taken similar steps toward better mental health. I hope that this book will give you a shoulder to rest on when life's stressors become too much so that someday soon, you'll be able to say "I've been there" without feeling ashamed or embarrassed.

Before we embark on this beautiful journey together and begin to explore ourselves in light of my therapeutic techniques, I want to lay out a few important facts to bust the bubble of the stigma that revolves around the concept of mental health. I know this will be hard to hear, but I can not emphasize it enough; emotional health is just as important as physical health. It's okay to want to learn how to handle your emotions. You're not broken or defective. You're just a person with feelings, and that's normal. People like us are the ones who make this world go round, and we deserve to be taken care of as much as anyone else does. When I was growing up, I experienced difficulty in managing my emotions. I thought of myself as having a problem with my emotions, and that caused me so much pain because I was ashamed of who I was. But now that I'm older and have seen the effects of mental illness in my life and the lives of others, it's clear that it's not something to be ashamed of at all; it's a part of who we are as human beings. So now, when someone asks if I'm having a bad day, instead of saying "No," which would make me seem apparently strong in their eyes, I say "Yes," even if it feels like more work than it should be. Because if there's anything we can do about our emotional health, let's do it together!

We need to stop stigmatizing the idea of therapy and mental health and start taking care of ourselves in a way that feels right for us. We have the right to seek help when we need it, and we should never see it as shameful or embarrassing to do so. We are all human beings, and it means that sometimes, our minds can't cope with the things going on in our lives. That doesn't mean we're broken or wrong for wanting to try something different from what we've always done before. It means we are human, and that means there is nothing wrong with seeking help when needed! So, remember that when you feel overwhelmed or scared, there are people who will always be there for you, and they're going through the same things as you! The sole purpose of my book is to provide my readers with a safe space where they can slowly work towards improving their mental health.

It's all about taking a deep dive into your emotions. By the end of this book, you'll be able to not only understand your emotional state but also find yourself efficiently managing the stressors that upset your mental well-being. You'll discover how this can make you emotionally healthy, not just for the short term but for good!

# Emotions

Emotions are the physiological and behavioral responses we have to things that affect our well-being. Evolutionary psychologists believe that emotions are a response to an external stimulus, a stimulus that is meant to guide an organism toward something good for its survival or reproduction. For example, when you see a lion in the wild, and it's time to run away from it, your brain releases hormones like adrenaline which causes you to run faster than usual. This response is adaptive because it helps you avoid danger. Similarly, when you feel sad after hearing about a loved one's death or during times of grief, your brain releases dopamine which can help you cope with these emotions by helping you focus on them less often so that they don't overwhelm you as much. Emotions are a powerful part of our experiences, and they help us to thrive and move forward in our lives. They are very important for our lives to help us make decisions and take action in certain situations. Emotions are like a switch that's turned on or off in our brains. On the one hand, emotions help us to feel things like pain or happiness. On the other hand, they also help us make decisions by helping us evaluate risks and rewards.

Why do we need emotions? Is it useful to have negative emotions? People have been asking these questions for decades, but in today's world, the answers aren't always clear. In this age of technology and instant gratification, we're bombarded with an endless stream of information about how to get things done. We're constantly told what we should do and how to achieve our goals. And in today's world, where there's no shortage of ways to accomplish your goals, you might think that it would be impossible to feel anything other than joy or happiness as you move forward towards them. But if you stop to think about it, what happens when you reach your goal? You feel good! You accomplished something! You worked hard and were able to do something meaningful for someone else! That must be why we have these positive feelings after accomplishing something; it's because we've accomplished something meaningful and worthy of celebration! But then, what happens when you fail at accomplishing something? You feel bad! You didn't succeed in doing what everyone else thinks is possible for you. And that can leave us feeling like failures, which is exactly why we need emotions like anger or sadness: they help us identify our shortcomings and pitfalls to come out stronger and better.

There was a time in my teenhood when I couldn't be the one to get a big kick out of my emotions. They were just so… messy. And I was always worried that someone would see them and think I'm a bad person. But the thing is, you aren't abnormal or wrong to feel all those negative emotions. You just have to know how to manage them and make them work for you. If you can do that, then negative emotions aren't so bad after all! The first step is to recognize when your negative emotions are happening. And the second step is figuring out how to use them in ways that help you and not hurt others. Let's say you're feeling anxious about something at school. The way we usually deal with anxiety is by attempting to avoid it by trying not to think about it or talk about it. But what if there were another way? What if, instead of running away from your feelings, you could find ways of engaging with them as part of your daily life? That's where mindfulness comes in, the practice of focusing on one thing at a time instead of being overwhelmed by everything at once (something we will explain later in detail).

# Common Emotions & Their Meanings

S o you're a human being, and you have emotions. That's normal. And sometimes those emotions can be negative. But what is the purpose of having them? It is because they help us to understand ourselves better. They teach us when something is wrong, and they help us to make better decisions in the future. If we weren't allowed to feel all of these things, then who would know what was bothering us? Who would be able to tell if something was wrong? We'd just keep walking around, not knowing how we felt because we weren't allowed any negative emotion at all, even when something felt wrong or frightening or just felt like "not enough." So maybe it's time for some change in our world: let's allow people to get sad or angry sometimes! Let's allow them to feel whatever it is that they want to feel! Let them know that it's okay for there to be a little pain in their lives sometimes. That way, when things are hard (and they will be), we will be able to courageously wade through the challenges of life instead of succumbing to our woes.

There are so many emotions that we go through in our life. Sometimes we feel happy, and sometimes we feel sad. Sometimes we're excited; sometimes, we're bored. Sometimes we feel angry, and sometimes we feel calm. To reiterate with an example, you probably know the feeling: you're at a party, and everyone's having fun. But then, suddenly, you start to feel super self-conscious and out of place. You feel like you have to go home, put your headphones on, and zone out. You can't help but feel depressed. You might think that this is just another moment in life where your brain has decided to take control of your emotions, but there's a lot more going on than that. The real story is much more complicated than just being sad or happy or angry or frustrated, for no apparent reason. Your brain may be controlling how you feel based on what it thinks will make you happy in the long run. Here's how it works: Your brain is constantly processing information from all over your body, your senses, for example, and using that information to predict what will happen next and how others around you will react to those events. It's an amazing system that allows us to survive as animals in groups without having to expend too much energy when something unexpected happens (like getting attacked by a bear). But our brains also do a lot more than just help us predict things: they also filter out negative experiences so that we don't have too many of them at any given time (which would make us sick).

I've learned to pay attention to the emotions that I feel because they tell me a lot about myself; what makes me tick and what makes me want to get out of bed on the morning of my birthday. The most important thing I've learned from all this is that no matter how much you try to hide it from yourself or others, your emotions are always going to be there, and it doesn't matter if they're deemed "normal" or not.

Let's paint a picture you're already familiar with (because if you weren't, you wouldn't be reading my book in the first place, right?) You're having a bad day. You're tired, and you've got too much on your plate to be dealing with this anxiety thing. You just want to get through it and go to bed, but then your brain starts going off in all these different directions, telling you that everything around you is going to end up falling apart or that someone out there is somehow going to make sure that everything around you falls apart, or even just something really simple like "I'm hungry." And then, Boom! An anxiety attack hits. Your heart starts pounding so hard you can feel it in your chest, and the world feels like it's moving in slow motion. You start getting lightheaded and dizzy, your arms feel heavy as lead weights, and it feels so difficult to breathe. It feels like someone else is controlling everything around you. It's almost like a voice in your head, a voice that tells you how awful everything is going to be if something doesn't change right away, but it's not a person talking at all; it's just this feeling that keeps rising inside of you. This is what a typical anxiety attack looks and feels like. But what's the mechanism behind our anxiety after all? Why do we end up feeling overwhelmed, stressed, nervous, restless, and afraid?

The short answer is that anxiety attacks are a way for our bodies to tell us something is wrong. Anxiety attacks are so common that most of us have experienced one at some point in our lives. The longer answer, however, is that anxiety attacks are an evolutionary response to danger, and it's a response that has served us well over the millennia. It's not just about helping you stay alive but also about keeping you healthy. Those who can stay calm during times of stress will be able to respond more effectively when things go wrong and therefore be more likely to survive and pass on their genes (which is why we're all here anyway).

When you get an anxiety attack, it can feel like the

world is ending. You might have a sense of dread and fear that something terrible is going to happen. You might not know what's causing your anxiety attack, but you feel like everything around you is falling apart, and you don't know how to stop it. For example, your friend calls you and asks if she can come over for dinner tonight. You're worried that she'll come here and like always, exaggerate about how much wealth she has and somehow ruin dinner by making fun of you. So now your anxiety has turned into a full-blown panic attack because, even though there's nothing bad happening in either case, both scenarios seem like disasters waiting to happen.

But here's the thing: It's never a fun time when you have an anxiety attack. But there are ways to treat your anxiety in a way that makes it easier to manage the symptoms and prevent future outbursts. First, try breathing exercises. This can help you calm down and focus on your breathing, which has been shown to reduce stress and anxiety levels. If you're having trouble with your breathing, try taking some deep breaths in through your nose and out through your mouth. Then repeat this for several minutes. You can repeat this as many times as needed until you feel calmer and more relaxed.

You can also try using a relaxation technique such as progressive muscle relaxation (PMR), which involves tensing and then relaxing different parts of your body slowly over time until all areas are calm and relaxed at once. You can do PMR by focusing on each muscle group or region of the body one at a time until they feel completely relaxed; then, move on to another part of the body until all areas are completely relaxed. Another way to help you manage your anxiety is by talking with someone who cares about you, someone who will listen without offering advice or judgment. These measures, of course, are coupled with an attempt to understand the root cause of your anxiety, which can prevent further emotional outbursts.

We've all been there. You and your friends are hanging out at your home, and one of them says something that just makes your heart filled with anger. But what's the point of an outburst? You know that if you get angry at them or start a fight, it will just make things worse for everyone. So, instead, what if we could somehow learn to use negative emotions as a tool? What if we could figure out how to harness that anger and resentment instead of letting it get in our way? It turns out there's a lot of science behind this idea, and psychologists have come up with some pretty cool theories about how we can learn to channel negative emotions into productive ones. So let's break down some of the key points: 1) Negative emotions are a signal from our bodies telling us we need something. Sometimes this is food; sometimes, it's sleep or water; sometimes, even just time off from study. Whatever it is, when your body tells you that you need something, you should listen! And 2) Negative emotions help us avoid danger by making us aware of potential threats before they happen and giving us the strength to deal with them if they do occur!

Anger, for instance, is a powerful emotion, one that can help you change your perspective or even motivate you to act on something you wouldn't normally do. Anger can also be a warning sign that something isn't quite right with the situation. Anger is often accompanied by other emotions like disappointment in ourselves or others, frustration, sadness, guilt, shame, and more. It's so important not only to recognize but also to embrace these feelings so that they don't become toxic ones that prevent you from moving forward with your life goals!

It's easy to get carried away with all the good feelings we have and forget that sometimes, it's important to feel annoyed or frustrated. It's important to feel angry, to let these emotions out, and let them work through our system. I remember when I was in high school, and my friend invited me over for a sleepover. She had just gotten a distinction in her final exams and wanted to celebrate that occasion with me. But since it was also my brother's anniversary that day, I wanted to go home early to be with my family. So I told her I had other plans for that day and went home instead of staying over at her house. Because I couldn't spend time with her, she got upset with me over it, and she would always get upset over these little things because of her emotional attachment towards me. But if she hadn't been so upset with me, she probably wouldn't have learned an important lesson about how important it is to feel empathy toward others and to give others their space. She did eventually learn this and our friendship thrived.

Feeling sad, depressed, disappointed, frustrated, hurt, embarrassed, mournful, jealous, or betrayed are emotions that can be caused by similar triggers. What's the psychology behind this sadness? Why do we feel sad, depressed, disappointed, and so on? There are many different causes of negative thoughts. The main cause for negative thoughts is stress or anxiety. When you have too much stress in your life, it can lead to mental disorders such as depression and anxiety. This can cause people to think negatively about themselves and their lives. When a stimulus is perceived as threatening to us, it activates the amygdala and hippocampus. The amygdala responds to threats by releasing hormones that make us feel anxious or fearful. The hippocampus helps us remember emotional events as well as encode our memories into neurons in the brain (remember: emotions = memory). So when you're sad about something that happened in your life that made you feel angry or betrayed, you remember how much it hurt you. Your brain is working overtime to help you see why those feelings are coming up!

So what can you do if this happens to you? You should be mindful of the negative emotions as they arrive because they're like messengers pointing towards a part of your personality that needs your attention! A friend or family member might be able to help and guide you to process these emotions. The first step is to acknowledge your negative emotions. When you notice negative thoughts or feelings, acknowledge them as they are happening. For example, when you are angry, rather than trying to push those thoughts away, acknowledge that you have anger and that it is ok to feel this way. It's important to be able to recognize the emotion at the moment so you can respond appropriately. The second step is to focus on what you can do about it. Rather than trying to get rid of your anger or worry about what other people think of you, take a moment to focus on what you can do about these feelings. For example, if you're worried about how others might perceive your choice of career or relationship, ask yourself if there might be another way for things to turn out differently than how they are currently going. If so, take steps towards making that change happen. The third step is self-compassionate action: taking care of yourself by being kinder towards yourself even when things are tough or not going well at all! You can do this by recognizing and accepting your feelings without judgment or criticism; honoring yourself with compassion; and taking action as necessary (e.g., getting support from friends and family).

All of these emotions have a similar underlying base: they are the consequences of the brain trying to protect itself from danger. The brain is constantly looking out for danger and trying to minimize the chance of it happening again. When we're scared or anxious about something (like being left alone in a dark room), our brains send out a signal that tells us to pay attention and look for potential threats. This can lead us to feel confused or unsure about what's going on around us, but it also helps us avoid danger. It makes perfect sense! This is why it matters so much that we understand how our brains work and why they behave the way they do. If we know how our brain works from an emotional standpoint (like feeling confused), then we'll be better able to manage those feelings.

I think it's important to understand that feeling negative emotions is not always a bad thing. I mean, I'm sure you've been advised to ignore your negative feelings. But I want to take a different perspective while handling such emotions. Because for me, those feelings were an important part of my journey toward becoming a better person. Understand that behind every emotion, there's a loophole behind it; sometimes, it's obvious, and sometimes you have to dig deeper. Like you, I also used to think that feeling negative emotions was a bad thing. I felt embarrassed by the fact that people would see me as weak, pitiful, or useless. But then I realized there's something really powerful about feeling those feelings and being able to work through them. It's not just about getting over them; it's about becoming stronger and more confident about it!

Sometimes we feel weak because we're scared of failing at something important: like taking a test, or making a new friend. But when you get into the habit of being honest with yourself and others about how you feel during these times, you can use that information to create new ways of thinking and acting. I'm not saying that everyone should go around saying "I'm useless!", but if you find yourself hesitant to face your fears because they make you feel like less of a person, give it some thought: could it be that there's something valuable in what those fears are telling us?

# 8 Steps to
# Self Regulation

When you're young, it's easy to get caught up in the moment. You have so much to learn, and the world is full of endless possibilities. But sometimes, all those things become too much, and instead of learning and growing, you just want to escape into a bubble where nothing can touch you. But no matter what your age, there are eight simple steps you can take to self regulate and manage your emotions to stay grounded when life gets overwhelming:

**1) Managing your reactions**: Communication is key, but it's not always easy to know what to say in a given situation. That's why we have to take a moment before reacting and think about the best way to respond. For instance, if your friend suddenly became angry at you during your class, try to find out what happened and what was the reason behind that incident so that you can better understand why your friend is acting this way. If you can't figure out what could have caused their actions, ask them! Remember, it's important to be empathetic and compassionate when possible. If someone is angry at you because of something that has nothing to do with you, listen and try your best not to take things personally (unless they say otherwise). Here's how it works: when you're angry or upset, stop and breathe! Take a moment to focus on your breath and the feeling of your chest expanding as you inhale. Ask yourself what emotions you are feeling and why. It's important to take a moment before reacting to think about how you want to respond. This will help you keep your cool and make sure that you're acting in line with your values and beliefs.

**2) Understanding your triggers**: Once you've stopped yourself from reacting impulsively, it's time to understand what set off those emotions in the first place. Was there something specific that happened? Or was it more of an overall feeling of uncertainty? Once you know where those triggers lie, it'll be easier for them not to trigger again in the future. It can be hard to know when your emotions are normal or if they're just a sign that something is wrong. It's normal to have different feelings at different times in your life, for example, when you're a teenager and the world feels very big and scary and confusing, but then again, as an adult, when we're capable enough to deal with the challenges of life, it can still feel that way. When you feel an emotion, it's important to acknowledge it instead of trying to push it away or ignore it completely (which will only make it worse). For example, if I'm feeling angry right now because someone cut me off in traffic, I need to take a deep breath and say out loud: "I'm angry." Then I'll try to figure out why I'm angry and how I can deal with that feeling without hurting anyone else by acting on it too quickly or harshly (which would make me feel even more frustrated).

**3) Empathizing**: Empathize with other people who are experiencing similar emotions as well! Talk about how difficult this must be for them, too; they may need someone else who understands what they're going through right now because nobody else does! Try to see things from the other person's point of view. This will help you understand what they're going through and why they might be upset. It'll also help you build a relationship with that person so that they feel like a friend or even family member, which will make them more likely to help you if you ever happen to need them as well.

**4) Accepting change**: You can't control everything

in life, so don't try; just accept it and move on. If someone says no to something, let it go and focus on other things in life instead of focusing on getting angry about it or feeling hurt by it (which will just make things worse).

**5) Overcome criticism:** Sometimes people aren't trying to criticize or hurt us when they say something seemingly rude; they just have different ideas about how things should be done! That's fine! Just remember that it's not personal; it just means they don't agree with us! It may be difficult at first, but try not to give in to these types of criticism; instead, learn how to deal with it healthily, so it doesn't affect your self-esteem or moods negatively.

**6) Setting Boundaries:** Boundaries are a good way to manage your emotions. They are the lines that you draw around the things that you just don't want to deal with, and they keep you from having to deal with them when it's not necessary. When we set boundaries, we're saying, "I don't want to do this," and "I don't want to feel this way." This is such an important skill for teenagers and adults because it helps them set their limits on what's acceptable and appropriate behavior. For example, if you're in class, and someone else keeps on trying to pass you notes while your teacher is giving the lecture, and you know it's not something that is respectful, you might want to wait until the class is over and then say something like, "I really need to get a good grade in this class , so I don't like to be distracted during the lecture" or "I don't need any problems with this teacher ,so please just wait until the he's finished talking to tell me something" Even then, if they don't stop bothering you in the class, it means that they'll have crossed a boundary. Setting boundaries is also important for managing our own emotions because it helps us avoid getting caught up in other people's problems or drama, or stress. You can't expect someone else to change for you if you don't show them respect by setting your limits. If someone does something that makes you uncomfortable, discuss your feelings to them and ask them to stop. If they don't listen, then walk away and don't return until they've taken the time to understand what's going on.

**7) Self-Care:** It's good to take a break from all the drama in your life once in a while. When things get too much, be sure to decompress and care for yourself by doing something that relaxes you or helps clear your mind. A hot bath, for instance, is always an excellent choice!

**8) Practicing:** You can't change over night, and should never expect to. This is why practice is the eighth and final step! You might not handle the next few stressful situations exactly how we've discussed in this book, but there's always next time. Never stop trying.

Before we dive into a detailed explanation of all these steps, it's important to know that not all situations in life require you to follow all 8 steps. But this process is a good foundation for managing emotions. When you're feeling overwhelmed and stressed, it can be hard to know what to do. But it's important to remember that every situation in life has its own set of emotions, and managing those emotions is a process that doesn't have to be rigidly followed. Here's how: Identify the emotion you're feeling or experiencing. You might feel angry, sad, or frustrated; for example, if your dog barks at you when you come home from a long day at school and you snap at it, this could be an expression of stress and agitation. Identify the thoughts or beliefs that are causing the emotion you're experiencing. These thoughts cause a lot of stress because they cause you to feel bad about yourself and your worth. The thought itself isn't necessarily wrong, but it creates an emotional response that perpetuates the stress cycle.

Consider what kind of coping skills will help you manage your response to the situation, and practice using them until they become automatic responses for you, and then stick with them! If you need to let go of a reaction that has been affecting your emotions (and causing distress), do so by identifying the part of yourself that is reacting strongly, rather than by focusing on the person or event itself because if we start to blame others for our reactions, we'll only amplify them! Instead, focus on identifying how this particular reaction makes sense within your wider context.

# STEP 1
# Managing Reactions

I've been there. I'll admit that sometimes I used to get frustrated with myself for not being able to control my emotions. It felt like I was constantly under a microscope, and I was trying to hide the fact that I feel things. It could be hard for me to be around people who don't understand what it's like to feel everything at once, the good and the bad, the happy and the sad. But you know what? That's okay! You don't have to worry about feeling bad if you feel something that makes you sad or angry or scared, you just do your best not to let those feelings control you, and then they'll eventually pass.

You might be thinking about how hard it is to make friends in school or how lonely it is to live in the city where everyone else seems so happy and no one will understand your thoughts and emotions. Maybe you're thinking about how many gifts your parents give you, yet fail to give you the attention you desire, and how they always seem to be busy, or maybe you're just wondering if you'll be able to pass your upcoming exams with good grades or not. Whatever it is that you're feeling right now, it's normal! It happens to everyone, even if we try not to show our feelings. The good news is that there's something that can help us manage our emotions better than anything else: communication! The more we talk about what we're feeling, the more likely it is that someone will understand us better than someone who doesn't know us very well at all.

When you're young, it's easy to get emotional. You've got a lot on your plate: life, relationships, school, friends, and more. And that's all before you even think about work. It can be hard to manage your emotions when you're so busy and stressed out. If a situation makes you angry or upset, take a step back and think about what happened before reacting in the first place. Why did it happen? Was there something else that led up to this moment? How can you use this information in the future? If something terrible happens (like being ditched by a friend), take time out for yourself so that you can process what happened and let go of whatever emotional state is making you feel sad. It's a pretty simple idea, but one that can make all the difference when it comes to regulating emotions. When we get angry, sad, or anxious, and we often do, we need to take deep breaths and remember that these feelings are temporary and not permanent. They're part of being human, and they'll pass.

Life is tough, and it can be particularly tough for teenagers. These are the years when we're still figuring out who we are and what our place in the world is. It's not always easy to find happiness or even to be happy. And something that makes this period of your life feel even more difficult is managing all the emotions that come with it.

Emotions can be overwhelming and confusing, especially when you're trying to figure out how to deal with them on your own! There's a simple practice to help you with this:

1) Identify your negative emotion and the way it makes you feel. Remember that feeling.

2) Name the feeling, so you can recognize it in the future.

3) Use that feeling as a reminder of how you want to be acting instead of reacting.

We all have to deal with our emotions, but they're not always easy to manage. Sometimes we feel like we just can't let loose and enjoy these feelings and that we might get hurt if we do. But this is nonsense! Your feelings are valid, and it's okay to feel them; you don't have to hold them in if you don't want to. You don't have to put on a happy face or make it look like everything is fine when something has gone wrong in your life that caused you pain or sadness. If someone has hurt you, or if a friend or loved one has done something that makes you feel angry or sad, it's normal for us to feel this way. Sometimes bad things happen, and we can't control them (for example, getting sick on a vacation and not being able to enjoy it), but other times something happens that makes us happy (like being randomly selected to win a prize at your work or school raffle). The point is that you can't always control what happens in your life, but you can control how you react.

I used to have a friend who was rude to me all the time. She'd get an attitude towards me for the smallest things, and it'd make me feel really bad about myself. At some point, I decided I'd treat her as rudely as she treated me, but quickly realized that getting mad at her wasn't going to solve anything; she knew she was being mean but couldn't stop herself thanks to her own personal traumas and an inability to handle her emotions. So I stopped caring about what she thought of me and tried to focus on myself. It worked! I started doing things for myself, like going to the gym or spending time with friends who were kind to me, instead of hanging out with her all the time, and it made me feel better about myself. After a few months, we had this big fight about something stupid, and I refused to allow her to yell at me and control the conversation like usual, so we ended up talking about our problems and agreed that neither one of us was right or wrong! Instead of reacting to her harsh words in a way that made me feel sad, or less than, I took a little control of the situation and it felt so good! No more yelling! No more hurting each other's feelings! She was shocked, at first, when I stood up for myself, but I could tell she understood why it had to be done. That's how important communication is in friendships and relationships. We both learned something from this experience: when you feel like something is wrong or unfair, just talk about it until you figure out what needs fixing!

We all deal with some form of anxiety at some point in our lives. It could be that you're nervous about an upcoming presentation at school, or it might be the fear of being unable to make friends. Whatever the case may be, it can be difficult to cope with this type of stress. Do you ever feel like there's something you should be doing? Like, if you just had some extra time and energy, you could do so much more. But then you realize that there never seems to be enough time or energy for everything. I used to feel this way too. And it wasn't until I started learning about psychology that I realized why: I was trying to solve my problems by overthinking them. This is what psychologists call "unhealthy coping mechanisms." A person with an unhealthy coping mechanism will use one of three methods to deal with stress: distraction, denial, and escape. A person who uses distraction to deal with stress often engages in activities that do not require him to think. They might watch television or play video games, for example. A person who uses denial is using a method of pretending that something does not exist or does not matter. For example, if a person has a problem fitting in and socializing, they may deny this problem exists by saying things like "it's no big deal" or "I'm too cool to be with other people." Escaping from reality by watching too much television or playing video games could also be considered an escape mechanism because this means you are withdrawing from your problems while still trying to cope with them in some way (i.e., denying reality). They are ways of solving problems that aren't solving them at all; they just make us feel better temporarily but don't help us solve our problems in the long run.

Coping mechanisms are a way of dealing with stress and anxiety that can either be healthy or unhealthy. The unhealthy mechanisms include behaviors such as substance abuse, overeating, or anger issues. These behaviors are often used by individuals who feel overwhelmed and out of control. For example, an individual may feel overwhelmed by their job or school work and resort to overeating, crying, or isolating themselves from their friends. This can lead to problems in their career or at school, which may cause them to feel even more stressed out about the situation. Or, a person might use avoidance as a coping mechanism when they are afraid of something or someone. They might avoid thinking about the thing or person, avoid talking about it, or even take steps to avoid their existence altogether. This is called "dissociation," and it's an unhealthy way of dealing with fear. If an individual refuses to eat dinner with his family every night and brings his plate to his room instead of sitting with his family, then he is likely using avoidance as a coping mechanism for stress or anxiety. Coping mechanisms can also be harmful, like becoming rebellious or eating a lot under stress. This can lead to addiction and other problems, including depression and anxiety. For this coping mechanism to become unhealthy, it must continue long enough for these consequences to occur.

And when we're in a situation where we feel like we have no control over our lives, it's easy to turn to these unhealthy coping mechanisms. These strategies might include bargaining with yourself: "If only I could get this or that thing, then everything would be okay," talking yourself out of doing something by saying "I'll do it tomorrow" or "It's not worth it," using avoidance mechanisms as a way of numbing yourself, so you don't have to think about anything that causes you pain, getting angry at other people for their behavior or attitude towards you because they make your life harder than it needs to be, instead of providing support when things get hard.

The problem with unhealthy coping mechanisms is that they can lead to a lot of emotional damage, even if you don't realize it at the time. For example, yelling can cause you to lose your voice, and your physical and mental health could also deteriorate. Yelling can make it very hard to communicate with others and can make it harder for you to get your point across. Another example is violence. If you are violent towards other people or yourself, this will likely cause problems with relationships in the future. People may not trust you because they've seen how abusive you are, and they may even feel unsafe around you. You might not be able to have friends or romantic partners because of these behaviors, which means that there isn't anyone who can support your feelings and help find solutions for them. A third example is throwing objects because it's easier than dealing with the emotions that might come up when speaking about what's bothering you. Throwing things helps temporarily take care of those emotions by distracting yourself from them instead of dealing with them head-on! But throwing things doesn't resolve anything; rather, it just keeps piling up anger and giving you more of a mess to clean up when you're done.

We all know that the more we try to hide our pain, the more it hurts in the long run. But what if we stopped hiding? What if we just let ourselves feel? You might be surprised at how much easier it is to stop pretending. You might also realize that feeling your feelings doesn't mean you're "weak," "emotional," or "unstable." It's often just the opposite! It means you're growing, learning, and becoming stronger every day, and that's something we should all be proud of. So, how do you start feeling your feelings? First, you can make space for yourself by pulling away from people and surroundings that make you feel like they're too much. This can be hard because we spend so much time trying to fit into other people's expectations of us, but this is your life! So, take some time for yourself every day and remember that you matter beyond what other people think about you. Secondly, you can also write down your thoughts and meditate over them so that when these thoughts arise, you're mentally prepared to handle their intensity.

To tell you the truth, growing up, I was never quite sure of the best way to cope with stress. I tried a lot of things: praying, meditation, and even running away from home. I was an expert at hiding out and pretending that everything was okay when it wasn't. My mother had a different approach. Instead of trying to distract herself or ignore her problems, she would try to face them head-on. For example, when she had a fight with my father, she didn't blame anyone for her struggles; instead she sat down and talked to my father about what was happening and how they could solve their problem without making any drama. And strangely enough, sitting with those uncomfortable emotions helped her healthily deal with that phase of her life.

Like all of us, I also used to think that I was going through a lot of things, but then I realized that maybe I wasn't. It turns out that all my problems were just a few minor inconveniences in my life. I was so caught up in them, though, that I didn't see the forest for the trees. I thought it was my fault that everything had gone wrong in my life, that if only I'd been more kind or more patient or more understanding, everything would have gone better for me. But now, having lived with this problem for a while, I realized very important things. I asked myself whether I should just keep trying to be happier? Should I keep trying to change myself? Or should I try to change everyone else around me? I realized that before changing others, it's important to change ourselves. And how do you know when you've changed enough? How do you know when you've done enough? It's hard not to feel overwhelmed by all of these questions. And it's even harder not to feel like giving up sometimes. But no matter how much pressure there is on us or how many things go wrong in our lives, it's important not to lose hope!

There's no denying that stress is part of life, and adopting unhealthy coping mechanisms is harmful to us. But the good news is that there are healthy ways to cope and manage it and make it more manageable. Walking away, for instance, is a great way to take a break from your problems. If you find yourself getting overwhelmed by them, take a break and go for a walk around the block or even in a park near your home. You'll come back refreshed, ready to tackle whatever it was that got you so emotional in the first place. It's also important to get enough sleep and eat healthy meals, but sometimes you just need some breathing room from other people or things, especially if those things have caused you stress in the past. Permit yourself to have time alone when you need it most! Meditation and deep breathing can be very helpful in relieving stress by helping you focus on what's happening around you instead of worrying about what might happen next (which can cause more stress). Try meditation exercises like abdominal breathing and progressive muscle relaxation once or twice per day, or try something like yoga, in general!

Another wonderful way to cope with stress is to do chores mindfully. Being in the present moment just clears your head, and helps you feel better. It's also great for your cognitive power to be mindful and present-minded! And if you're feeling overwhelmed by something in your life that's making you feel bad, talk to your loved ones about it. You might feel better afterward and maybe even feel capable of dealing with whatever is overwhelming you!

Interestingly, it's a common misconception that stress is only associated with unproductive situations. That's not entirely true! Stress can be both productive and unproductive, depending on the situation. For example, when you're trying to meet a deadline at work, it's generally considered productive stress to be nervous about getting it done on time. But when you're feeling overwhelmed about year-end accounting reports that are due in December, and it's only February, that might be an indication of unproductive stress. What matters is how much pressure you're feeling and whether or not it's making it hard for you to get anything done. The same thing goes for school; you may feel stressed about getting good grades in your classes, but if the class itself isn't giving you any trouble, and instead you're worried about your classmate getting a higher grade than you, then it's probably unproductive stress! Constantly trying to get the highest grade in class is unnecessary stress when the main goal should be doing well! You should always try to evaluate what kind of stress is getting in the way of you achieving your goals or accomplishing other tasks at hand to make your stress productive and fruitful.

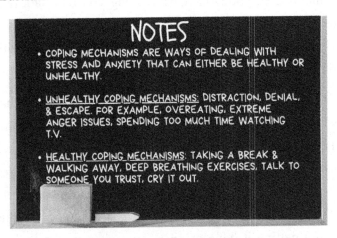

NOTES

- COPING MECHANISMS ARE WAYS OF DEALING WITH STRESS AND ANXIETY THAT CAN EITHER BE HEALTHY OR UNHEALTHY.

- UNHEALTHY COPING MECHANISMS: DISTRACTION, DENIAL, & ESCAPE. FOR EXAMPLE, OVEREATING, EXTREME ANGER ISSUES, SPENDING TOO MUCH TIME WATCHING T.V.

- HEALTHY COPING MECHANISMS: TAKING A BREAK & WALKING AWAY, DEEP BREATHING EXERCISES, TALK TO SOMEONE YOU TRUST, CRY IT OUT.

# Journal Prompts

The following questions are intended to help you get a sense of how emotionally reactive you are. This is completely voluntary, but it will help you understand what makes you feel and react the way you do, plus it just helps to write out your feelings! Grab a notebook that you can use as a journal, or write your answers in the note app on your phone. Reflect on your responses and use them as a tool during your journey to healthy emotional management!

1) How do you feel when someone says something negative about your quirks/ eccentricities? What is typically your first reaction when this happens?

2) When someone asks "how was your day?", how often do you feel the urge to smile and say "fine", even though you had a rough day? What keeps you from being truthful about your feelings when someone asks this question?

3) Do you feel the urge to yell when being in a tense discussion? If so, why do you think this happens?

4) What's a healthy coping mechanism you plan to implement in your life whenever you feel angry, sad, or stressed (for example, walking away and taking a breather when you feel the urge to yell, or finding someone you trust to talk to when you have a bad day, rather than bottling your feelings)?

# STEP 2
# Understanding Triggers

Emotional triggers are a type of memory that we all share. An emotional trigger can arise from something as simple as listening to music you may have bad memories from, or as complex as watching someone being bullied. We may not always be aware of them, but they are there. When we experience an emotional trigger, it can cause a flood of memories to come rushing back at us, often with intense emotion. Such strong emotions are triggered by external events or internal thoughts and feelings. External events can be anything from seeing a loved one or thinking about a person who has died, to hearing music that reminds us of someone who has gone away. Internal thoughts and feelings include our moods, past experiences and beliefs about ourselves. Emotional triggers can result in strong feelings such as grief, sadness, or anger that last for many days or weeks after the original event. They can also cause physical symptoms such as stomach aches, headaches or nausea if we're not ready to deal with our emotions at this time in our life. Emotional triggers can be intentional or accidental. Some examples of emotional triggers are: being embarrassed when someone points out your poor grades; seeing someone else crying, which makes you feel uncomfortable; feeling excessively upset when you hear about a death because your pet just passed away, etc.

The causes of emotional triggers are varied but can often be traced back to childhood experiences or trauma. Some people feel too much emotion at once; still, others feel disconnected and numb from their feelings; both of these scenarios can lead to depression or anxiety disorders. But the point is; that we all have them; the things that make us feel a certain way, in certain situations, that we think will never go away. Some are more obvious than others, but they're all around us; they're just waiting to be noticed by someone ready to recognize them and work through them.

The way we respond to those emotions can impact our mental and physical health. For example, if you're angry, your heart rate and blood pressure increase. This can lead to high blood pressure and other cardiovascular problems like stroke or heart attack. Anger also raises your blood sugar levels, which can cause other health issues. If you're sad, your immune system may weaken because of a hormone called cortisol. Cortisol is used by the body when it's under stress or threat of danger such as when you're sad or depressed. This hormone is said to weaken the immune system and make you more susceptible to infections and illness. The effects of emotional triggers on mental health can also be devastating. When we experience setbacks in life, they may bring up feelings of failure and sadness. These feelings can cause us to doubt our abilities or feel like we are not good enough as a person. Our emotions can stay with us for days or weeks after the setback occurs. If the setback is big enough, it may cause us to stop doing things such as working out or socializing because we do not want others to notice that we are not feeling well.

The first step to working through an emotional trigger is to recognize it exists at all. Once you've identified it, you can begin to take practical actions: Try patting your shoulders with your arms if loneliness begins to feel triggering; eat ice cream (in moderation) when you need comfort food; watch a movie or TV show that reminds you of happy times in your childhood. These "emotional triggers," things like music, food, movies, or TV shows that remind us of something specific about our childhood can also prompt a positive emotion like nostalgia or even happiness! But sadly, we're mentally designed to think about emotional triggers as reminders of times when we didn't have control over our feelings. These are the kinds of memories that make us feel powerless but they can never snatch from us the power to determine what feelings we want to choose and what feelings we want to discard at the end of the day.

Emotional triggers are anything that can elicit an emotional response in you. They can be positive or negative, but they're all-powerful. For example, if you're having a conversation with someone and they ask you a question like "How was your day?" and you respond by saying, "It was depressing," you might've triggered them to be responsible about how you are feeling. It may not be a socially accepted custom, but such honesty can definitely strengthen the bond between you two because your communication will be based on honesty and compassion. That's a good thing! It means that you trusted that person enough to answer honestly. Trust and honesty are what ultimately we all desire from our relationships, but not everyone is ready to handle such responsibility, so such openness can be very triggering for many. You might have experienced this trigger yourself when someone opened up to you about negative feelings they were having.

Sometimes, our emotions can be triggered by things we don't even realize are triggers. It could be the reason a frustrated individual yells at you, or why your friend is mean to you, for seemingly no reason. These kind of triggers happen in flashbacks and recurrent experiences, and it's a little difficult to sort them out. This has always made me feel like there must be some kind of "deep" reason for why we react to things in different ways, like how we react to someone who makes us mad is no different than how we react to someone who makes us sad. But I realized those feelings are just different ways of being triggered. If you're sad, you might have a thought like, "I'm not pretty or intelligent" This is an emotional trigger. It makes you feel sad, and its root cause can be dated back to your childhood experiences and your connections with your family and friends. The same goes for anger or frustration. Whenever you feel pushed into a socially awkward situation, for example, you might think, "I'm angry at the world," or "I want to punch something." These emotions are triggered by your fear of being in a crowd. Emotional triggers can be good or bad things, but their validity and effect in our personal or professional lives is not something to forget about!

A friend of mine was telling me about the time he met a girl at a dance and ended up falling in love with her. She was so beautiful and fun, but when they got to know each other better, it seemed like she had a lot of anger issues and she would get triggered over the smallest of things. He was trying to be cool and not make a big deal out of it, but as soon as he told me about a few situations that had occurred, I could tell he was feeling stuck with her because he didn't have the courage to speak to her about his feelings. It's easy to overlook small things like this when you're in a rush of life, but it's also important for us to understand that if these triggers are not dealt with right away, they'll keep piling up and someday cause a lot of damage to the person holding those issues and to his or her loved ones. So, we need to understand what emotional triggers are in their true face, so we can take care of ourselves when we're under pressure. These triggers appear as little things that might upset emotions in us, but in truth they exist because they remind us of feelings or experiences we've had before, which were traumatic in a way. These triggers can either be harmless or a cause of full-blown episodes, depending on how much they affect our past. For example, if someone stops talking or gets angry all of a sudden, when you mention stories about your father, it may be an indication that that person has unpleasant memories relating to his familial life. But there's nothing wrong with having an emotion triggered by something like this; it just means that person has a functioning physiological and mental state, and believe me when I say that going numb towards our bad experiences is a lot worse than feeling their pangs once in a while.

Feelings, in their true nature, are visceral experiences that happen right away and aren't reasoned out over time or thought out carefully beforehand (like being asked questions). Emotional triggers that you experience are caused by the way your brain works, and the way your brain works is not always obvious. The first thing to remember about emotional triggers is that their nature can be both simple or complex. For example, if someone holds something in their hands when they're feeling anxious, like a pen or a pencil, that hand-holding can become an automatic way to calm down and relax. But sometimes, we find it hard to breathe in a socially awkward situation. We don't even realize how our unconscious behaviors affect us until we see them reflected in the outside world around us! Why do we feel happy or sad? Why do we get angry? When a classmate calls or sends you an email to meet in person, why do you feel anxious? And why does it take such a long time for our feelings to change? It's not just something that happens to you but everyone. It's something you can control. You can choose whether to be happy or sad, angry or calm; you can decide how your emotions will affect your life and those around you.

This is where I believe the science of emotion comes in: understanding how your emotions work and why they're important is key to being able to control them better. Emotional triggers can be caused by a variety of factors, including stress, trauma, or other experiences. They can also be caused by external events and circumstances, such as family situations or other people in your life. If you're having trouble identifying what is causing your emotional triggers, it might help to think about how you feel when you experience them. For instance, does the thought of that 'one' person make you feel anxious? Do you get upset when they call? Do you feel sad when you think about them? Think about how these emotions make you feel in your body; are they more physical or more mental? Are they more intense than others? Do they last longer than others? Once you've identified the types of triggers that are affecting you most often, try to identify why those feelings are happening. For example, you might be feeling angry because of a person's rude remark towards you or because your best friend ghosted you for no reason. Once you've identified why these feelings are happening, it'll be easier to figure out how to change them. You might need to talk with someone or take some time away from certain people or places to work on your triggers.

So, how do we go about making peace with our emotional triggers? How do you know when you're being triggered from a traumatic cause? It's a question that has plagued us for a long time, but one that can be answered in just a few simple steps. First, step back and try to identify what's triggering you. You'll need to be able to articulate your emotions so that they can be translated into discernible language. For example, if you're feeling angry about something, it could be helpful for you to ask yourself, "What am I feeling?" or "Why am I angry in this particular situation?" Next, take a look at the situation that is causing your emotional distress. Is there any way to change it? If not, then the key lies to learning how to go through that situation without losing your guard. If there is a way to change it, if there are things that can be done differently, then now might be a good time to do those things! Finally, try not to get sucked back into the emotional spiral of worry and anxiety. Instead of dwelling on the problem (and therefore making it worse), focus on what works! For example, maybe taking some deep breaths will help calm down.

If I'm feeling anxious, I might find myself staring at

the clock and diving into my world of imagination or doing a bunch of quick tasks to try to distract myself. If we keep this in mind when we notice ourselves getting anxious or upset, we can start looking for the things that trigger these feelings. For example, if you're the kind of person who can't complete his homework in time and ends up feeling embarrassed in front of the teacher, figure out what aspect of your life is causing you to become lazy and causing your lack of interest in the things that matter. There's nothing wrong with that; we just need more awareness so that we're prepared when these things happen! Another way to identify our emotional triggers is to look at how we respond to the things in our lives that we find difficult or unpleasant. For example, if you are upset by a comment made by your teacher, it's probably a good idea to take a step back and consider why you might be reacting so strongly. What's the biggest thing that happened recently that could have triggered this reaction? Was there something else going on in your life recently? What was your relationship with your teacher before this interaction? If you're not sure what triggered this reaction, just ask yourself: "What am I feeling right now?" The answer might lead you to some new information about yourself (or about your teacher) that will help you figure out why you reacted so strongly.

Emotional triggers of teenagers are oftentimes misunderstood by adults. Teenagers are particularly vulnerable to the effects of these triggers because they are still developing their own identities and self-esteem, which is why it's so important that they have a strong support system in place. The most common emotional triggers for teenagers include bullying and abuse, which can lead to depression and anxiety disorders. While these issues are difficult for anyone to deal with, they can be especially devastating for teenagers who are already struggling with schoolwork or other aspects of life. Triggers that are most harmful to teenagers are those that come from the outside world. These can be things like peer pressure, family dysfunction, or even just bad experiences with teachers and other authority figures.

You're not a robot, so why do emotional triggers feel like they're controlling your behavior and making you do things that you regret? It's because emotional triggers are a form of conditioning. They cause people to act in certain ways, even when they don't want to. These emotional triggers can be anything from a song on the radio to a smell that reminds you of someone who's gone. The more we try to avoid them, the more they seem to intrude in our lives. And if you've been conditioned by an emotional trigger, it's hard to shake it off. You might be able to talk yourself into taking a shower or brushing your teeth when you feel like it, but what happens when that trigger comes up, whether in your mind or in real life? A lot of times, people will try avoiding these triggers by trying not to think about them or avoid situations where they might happen again. But this just makes them worse! Avoiding them only makes them more powerful than ever before! Instead of trying to avoid feeling something, try focusing on the good parts of your life instead! Emotional triggers are a big part of the reason that people can't just "get over" things. There are times when our emotions do serve us well— we're happy, we feel love, we're optimistic, and then there's the other side of the coin: the side where we feel pain, sadness, anger, frustration, a whole host of unpleasant feelings that we don't want to deal with. And this is where emotional triggers come into play. If you're feeling angry or frustrated about something, it's easy to snap at someone who makes you feel that way. It's also easy to take out your frustration on yourself by eating too much junk food, almost like a punishment. Emotional triggers not only make it easier for us to act on our emotions in unhealthy ways; they can also be harmful to our physical health, for example, by causing us to gain an unhealthy amount of weight if we overeat in response to these triggers, and put ourselves at risk for a plethora of health issues.

That being said, I also believe that emotional triggers can prove a helpful tool for teenagers, who are often confused and overwhelmed by their emotions. They can be used to help teens understand what they're feeling and why. For example, if a teen feels sad because of a fight with his/her best friend, he or she might get triggered in the form of panic attacks if that person has separation anxiety, or he/she may get addicted to things like listening to sad music or watching dramas to fill the void. But if they understand their triggers, they'll realize that they're actually feeling a loss of love. This realization can help them process the pain of the loss and express it healthily. I also believe that emotional triggers can help teens understand the importance of taking care of themselves when they feel overwhelmed by emotions. For example, if you are feeling angry at your parents for not giving you enough money for college fees, you may want to listen to angry music or watch an action movie with lots of explosions, but these responses can create violent tendencies in you. But If you respond to these triggers by, say, working part-time to handle the college fees, not only will you feel independent and self-reliable but these activities will help you take care of yourself and your needs. But I understand that teenagers have a hard time getting out of their mood swings, from the highs of excitement to the lows of depression. While it's true that teenage hormones can make it difficult for them to keep their emotions in check, there are some ways you can help yourself manage your emotions. And from all the ways that I've mentioned, understanding your triggers is the most reliable way to manage your emotions and make sure you stay on the right track.

When you're a teenager, it can be hard to get the emotional support you need. And it's not just because your parents are busy with work or school, or that your friends are busy with their own lives. It can also be because your friends have been through so much already and they have no time to help you deal with your problems. That's why I think we should always give others a greater edge. When I was growing up, we had a weekly meeting called "The Talk." It was where parents would talk to their kids about what they were going through in life so that they knew how to help each other when times got tough. I think this could be done for teens as well. Teenagers deal with a lot of stress, and sometimes it's hard for them to find someone who understands them on a personal level. If we created a place where teens felt comfortable talking about how they felt without being judged or ridiculed, this could be valuable for many people, especially those who may not have any family members or friends who understand them well enough to listen without making assumptions about what they might need or want from the situation at hand. If parents are reading this book in hopes of helping their children manage their emotions, you might also think of events like watching a movie together or going out with friends as an example. Your teenager will most likely remember these things whenever they feel like they're having trouble controlling their emotions. By setting up an environment where your teen feels safe, loved, and understood, you'll be able to help them find new ways of managing their emotions. Try setting aside time once a week just for hanging out with them and, if possible, try to include other family members in these activities too! But first, parents need to know how to deal with these issues so that they can help their children heal from past wounds. They should also be aware of what signs indicate an issue might be present in their child's life so that they can intervene before problems escalate too far.

Now, let's talk about a severe, albeit common, form of emotional trigger that causes phobias in teenagers. Phobias in teenagers are quite common. They can be triggered by many things, but the main cause is often the way a person was raised. For example, if your parents have phobias, you may inherit them and have them too.

Many people think that phobias are just a result of bad memories and traumatic experiences. However, this is not always true. Some phobias are caused by genetics and hormones.

Phobias are also caused by an event or situation that is extremely frightening to a person. The fear is usually triggered by a thought, memory, or emotion that was experienced at some point in the past. It can also be triggered by something that a person has seen or heard about on television, in movies, or from friends. There are several different types of phobias, including social, situational, and health-related. Social phobias are triggered by the thought that you'll be judged or ridiculed due to your appearance or behavior. Situational phobias occur when you're exposed to something that causes a strong emotional response. Health-related phobias are triggered by a specific situation that could lead to an accident or illness. Teenagers can suffer from any type of phobia including: 1) Agoraphobia - Fear of open spaces. 2) Hoarding - Fear of discarding things or having too much stuff around them. 3) Social Phobia - Fear of embarrassing oneself in front of others (social anxiety) 4) Nomophobia - Fear of being alone (loneliness). While many teens have fears of being alone, being in public places, or being around large groups of people, others may be afraid of spiders, snakes, or other animals.

I remember the first time I realized I had a phobia of the dark. As an adult, I still slept with a nightlight and could rarely go to sleep in complete darkness. I, eventually, learned that this fear began when I was young, after my family and I moved into a big house in the country, and I was very lonely in this huge, new, space. My dad used to come home from work and read me stories every night until I went to sleep, but now that he worked so far away, it seemed like he was gone all day every day. For a while, we didn't have any lamps in our rooms, so it was always dark. It felt like my sister and I were trapped inside! We had no way of knowing if there were any animals nearby who might be looking for food or shelter and if they did find us, what would they do? Would they hurt us? Would they eat us? Would we even recognize them as an animal at all (remember, these are the irrational thoughts of an 8 year old)? Deep down, I knew that these thoughts weren't rational, but I just could'n't make them go away. We eventually got lamps in our room, but something I noticed is once my dad's long work hours changed and he started coming home from work early again, I rarely needed to sleep with lights. This makes sense because, as an adult, one of the main times I required a nightlight was when I felt alone in the world. It wasn't until I came across cognitive and exposure therapies to overcome my phobia when I realized my life was pretty much revolving around these fears. You might be surprised by how much control we have over our mental health. Many people think that their thoughts or feelings are just "how life is", but they're not! It's our job as humans to choose what we pay attention to, and how we react to those thoughts and feelings. The next time you feel overwhelmed by stress, remember that there is always something you can do to change the way things look from the inside out. It starts with making small changes in your behavior and taking the time to learn yourself.

People with phobias often find themselves unable to cope with situations that would otherwise be manageable because of their fear; as a result, they avoid those situations altogether. For many, phobias and triggers can be treated effectively through cognitive therapy and exposure therapy. Cognitive therapy teaches sufferers how to change their thoughts about their anxiety-producing triggers; exposure therapy helps them face those triggers in a safe environment and practice coping skills until they become accustomed to them. Cognitive therapy is a form of psychotherapy that uses a person's own thoughts and behaviors to help them understand themselves and their emotions, which can then be used to treat phobias. Exposure therapy is a type of psychotherapy in which people are exposed to their phobic situation in small increments until they can face it without any anxiety. When you're first starting this process, it can feel like you're walking through a minefield, but once you get the hang of it, it will become easier and easier to manage. So what do you need to do? First and foremost, figure out what's causing your trigger or fear. Take a deep breath and think about what happens when you're afraid—what does that feel like? What would happen if these things happened? If you don't know how to answer these questions, look up some resources online or talk to a counselor. Once you know what's causing these feelings, then it's time to tackle it head-on! You'll need tools like breathing exercises and visualization techniques (like imagining yourself doing something without actually doing it) so that when the time comes for your next panic attack or anxiety attack, you can use those tools instead of letting them overwhelm you.

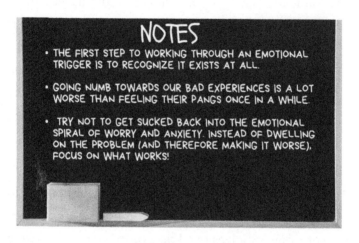

# Journal Prompts

1) Name at least 1 of your triggers and why you think you have it? For example, one of my triggers is being criticized. Through therapy, I learned that this was one of my triggers because, as a child, I had "tiger parents" who constantly pushed me to be the best and they criticized me much more than praised me. So, as an adult, anytime someone gave me the smallest criticism, I couldn't handle it.

2) What strategy do you plan to implement in order to better handle this trigger? In my case, now when someone criticizes me, I take deep breaths and listen to them. Then, I remind myself that everyone is entitled to their opinion, and an opinion can't hurt me; an opinion does not mean I'm a failure. Also, once I feel more calm, I ask myself if there is any truth to that opinion and how I can improve, if so.

3) Is there anything/anyone in your family that makes you uncomfortable or triggers your emotions?

4) Have you ever tried to face your emotions, however triggering they may be? If yes, how did that experience feel? If not, why not?

# STEP 3
# Learning Empathy

You're a teenager, and you've probably been struggling with managing your emotions for a while now. Maybe you are often angry, or maybe you sometimes feel like your anger is out of control. You might have even tried to talk to someone about it before, but they just didn't understand what you were going through. Empathy means understanding another person's feelings and perspectives by taking into account those feelings and perspectives. So, the first step is to imagine yourself in their shoes, to picture how it feels when they are having an emotion, how you would feel if you were experiencing that emotion, and how your actions might affect them. What if you could tell your parents, "I don't understand why you're so mad at me right now"? What if you could tell your friends, "I'm sorry for overreacting in the past"? When we get emotional, we tend to be more focused on ourselves; we think about how we feel, what we want from others, and what it would mean for us to get those things. But when we start to consider the perspective of others, when we stop thinking about ourselves and start thinking about how other people might feel, we begin to see them in a new light. It opens our hearts up so much more than if we just kept running up against walls that were made of stone. This is especially important for teenagers and young adults because they often have trouble understanding the emotions of others (especially those who are different from them). But with empathy, they can learn how to manage their own emotions better by understanding those around them.

They say that the most important thing in life is empathy and compassion. I believe it. I'm a big proponent of empathy and compassion. They're important not just for your health and wellness but also for the well-being of others. Empathy can also be described as the ability to understand another person's emotions or experiences. Compassion is the ability to feel another's pain and suffering or to have the desire to relieve that pain. Empathy and compassion are built into our brains; we're hard-wired for it! We all have neural circuits that make us more likely to empathize with people who are in similar situations (for example, if you're feeling sad, you're more likely to feel sadness for someone else who's sad) and less likely to empathize with people who are in different situations (for example, if someone is feeling happy, you're less likely to feel happy for them). We also have neural circuitry that makes us more likely to be compassionate when we see someone in pain; it doesn't matter if they deserve it or not; we just want them better! And there's no better way than by helping them do what they need (whether it's taking care of themselves by eating right or getting help from a friend).

However, if you find yourself unable to empathize with others, don't panic! You're not alone. Empathy is a skill that can be learned and improved with practice, and it's something that everyone is capable of developing. But what if you find that you just don't have the ability to put yourself in someone else's shoes? Don't worry! It's totally normal—and even expected! After all, we all have different experiences and backgrounds that shape our worldviews. Some of us were raised in homes where our parents encouraged us to think more deeply about how we were treated by other people; while others were raised in homes where they were told to treat others as they would want to be treated (which may or may not include thinking about how others may feel). So, if you don't feel like you can put yourself in someone else's shoes, don't beat yourself up about it! It's not an indication that you're less empathetic than everyone else, it just means that your experience has been different from most people's experiences.

Teenagers feel like they have everything wrong with them: their parents don't understand them or understand their problems, their friends don't want anything to do with them, their teachers are boring and uncreative, and the list goes on. But this feeling won't last forever—you just need to remember that no matter how hard things seem right now, it's only temporary. The first step in overcoming feelings of apathy and hatred is realizing that you're not hopelessly lost in the world—it's okay if you don't understand this one thing or another right now, but we promise that things will get better soon! Start by taking a deep breath (or three) and reminding yourself that there's nothing wrong with being confused or scared right now—that's perfectly normal! Then try asking someone who cares about you for advice or help when needed. There's always someone out there who will listen!

It is not easy to live in a world where there is so much hate and apathy. We can't do anything about it, but we can try to regulate our own feelings. It is important for us to learn how to manage our feelings so that we don't get affected by what other people say or do. The first step is by accepting ourselves for who we are and learning how to accept others as well. We need to start with ourselves. We should try to understand why we feel the way we do and find out if there is something wrongt. If there is something wrong then try to change that thing because change starts from within us! We need to show love towards everyone in this world, even if they have done bad things or hurt us in any way possible. It is empowering to forgive someone, forget about the past and move forward with your life without holding grudges against anyone who did wrong things toward you. Instead of feeling powerless, try working on your self-esteem. It will help you know that you are worth something. You won't be so easily influenced by the things people say to you, or how they think of you. You can also try working on your self-confidence by doing things that make you feel good about yourself.

Have you ever heard the saying, "Empathy is the most powerful tool for change"? Well, I think it's true. After learning this, I started paying attention to other people's stories and expressions when they talked about those things that made them feel different or sad, the same way that psychologists recommend we do in therapy sessions.

I have always been the kind of person with many goals, and I worked hard to achieve them. But one day,

I realized that something was missing from my life: a true connection with others. I felt isolated and alone, even though I was surrounded by friends and family. It's not like they didn't care about me; they did! But it didn't feel like enough. One day, after being diagnosed with an illness that required me to take time off work for treatment, I decided to go on a retreat in hopes of reconnecting with myself and learning how to better care for myself physically and emotionally. During this time, I met several people who had similar experiences as me, people who suffered from chronic pain or illnesses that made their lives difficult. These people taught me more about compassion than anything else could have done (even though we didn't always see eye-to-eye). They showed me that there are many different ways of being human, and each person on this earth has unique gifts that make them special!

Empathy and compassion are important for our lives because they help us to connect with others, which in turn helps us to feel better about ourselves. Empathy and compassion are also important because they help us create a better world for everyone around us, for example, by making sure that there are safe spaces for those who need them (like at schools) or by working toward equality in society so that everyone has access to resources like education or healthcare just like anyone else does (like at work).

We are all connected in the world, and we all have a part to play. If you're like me, you've probably heard this time and time again. But what does it mean? What does it take to be fully connected? I think it's about empathy and compassion—both of which I believe are so important for our lives because they help us see the world through other people's eyes. Empathy is when we recognize that the things that happen to others are just as important as the things that happen to us. Compassion is when we understand how our actions affect those around us, even if they aren't always easy or pleasant to experience. I think these two traits are essential not only because they make life easier for everyone around us but also because they allow us to see ourselves in others and make connections between ourselves and others. I believe that when we all work toward being more empathetic and compassionate toward each other, we can truly achieve happiness as individuals and in communities.

We need both empathy and compassion in our lives because, without them, we wouldn't be able to see things from another person's perspective or understand their emotions. Without compassion, we'd be unable to help someone else who was suffering or in pain. And without empathy, we wouldn't know how to relate to others on a deeper level; we might even become frustrated with them if they didn't seem like they were getting what we wanted from our interactions with them! Empathy is key for helping us build strong relationships with others by making it easier for us to connect and understand each other's needs. We can't do this if we don't understand each other's feelings on an emotional level, and being able to put ourselves in someone else's shoes helps us do just that! People want to be around open-hearted people. But you can't just say that; you have to act it out. You can't just tell someone they're being too closed-hearted. You have to find a way to make them want to open up their hearts, and then make them feel like you're feeling it too, and then you have to show them that you mean it. If you want someone to open up their heart, there are a couple of ways to go about it: first, ask questions like "What do you think about this?" or "How would you solve this problem?" That way, they'll get the chance to talk about whatever they're thinking or feeling without having to worry about your judgment of it. The second way is by asking someone if they would ever consider doing something new or different with their life. This will allow them not only to talk about how they feel but also what kind of changes could potentially happen in their lives if things change around them at all levels (social, emotional, physical).

I think the key is to step back and observe yourself. Take some time out of your busy day to sit down and just observe how you feel about others. What do you notice? Is it that you're not as kind or caring as you could be? Or are you noticing that it's not so much that you're not being kind and compassionate, but rather that your compassion is limited? It's easy to say, "oh, I'm going to try harder," but the truth is that it takes a lot of practice to learn to be more open toward others. For example, if someone asks for help with something, do not say "no." Instead, ask them how they would like to handle things themselves. Sometimes, people need space from other people for them to work through their issues in their way. So, by giving them space, we show others that we trust them enough to give them this space when they need it!

The first thing to understand about empathy is that it's not something you have; it's something you do. Empathy isn't an innate quality; instead, it's a practice. And like any other practice, there are specific steps you can take to make sure that your efforts yield results. Empathy begins with being aware of your own emotions and those of others. This means paying attention to what people say and do and taking note of their reactions to different things throughout the day. It also means noticing when someone is sad or angry and asking yourself, "what could give this person the feeling that I just saw?" Once you realize that people feel different things in different situations, it will be easier for you to empathize with them. The next step is being able to understand why someone might feel one way rather than another. This may sound difficult at first, but once you start paying attention to what people are saying and doing around you, it becomes easier and, even more importantly: natural!

There are so many ways you can practice empathy in your everyday life as a teenager. Here are just a few: When you're walking home from school, take the time to notice how people's lives look from their perspective. You might see a homeless person on the street, or maybe someone is just walking hopelessly around with headphones on, listening to music. Try to picture yourself in their shoes. Take the time to talk to someone who seems upset about something, but don't ask them why they're upset! Just listen to what they have to say and ask questions if you want. It might help them feel less alone or like they're not crazy for feeling how they do. If you happen upon someone who seems sad or upset, offer them a kind smile; it might make them feel better!

Considering someone else's perspective is very important in our journey to manage our own emotions.

You can't always understand your friend's perspective or point of view, but you can make an effort to try. Here are some things you should consider: Is it possible that you don't understand their perspective because they're not clear? Ask them why they think it's important to say what they say, and ask them to explain any unclear parts of their message. If you do understand their perspective, does it make sense to you? Are there things about their reasoning that don't line up with your own? Or is there something about the way they frame their argument that doesn't make sense to you? Are there pieces of information that could help you better understand the other person's thinking? Maybe they're making a lot of assumptions based on limited information; maybe it would be helpful if they made a list of those assumptions and then explained how they came to those conclusions. The point is to consider these things before jumping to a conclusion.

It's easy to get lost in the world of social media. We all know what's going on, and we all see our friends' lives through their posts and status updates. But what about when you're trying to truly understand someone? It's easy to feel like you can understand them through what they post on social media. But be open minded with your reactions. You'll never know what actually happens behind the curtains of social media- in real life.

So don't judge them on the way they post on social media, but instead try to find out about their real lives! Try not to take things personally. This is hard, but remember that lots of people have hard days right now, and they might not even realize it themselves yet! And be kind! It's so easy to be mean online, but it doesn't help relationships or help anyone get anywhere. Instead of being judgmental, try being supportive, and remember that everyone has their way of doing things and their reasons for doing things that you may never fully understand.

There's a lot to learn in life, but what if you could learn it all from the perspectives of others? What would it be like to have a different point of view? To see the world through someone else's eyes? To hear about someone else's experiences and see how they're different from yours but also similar? You might think that knowing what it's like to be someone else would make you feel less alone in your skin. But I'm here to tell you that it requires courage to have this power inside your heart. Empathy is a little tricky because we can never really get inside someone else's head, and yet we need to understand them if we want to get along with them. It's not that straightforward to put yourself in another person's shoes and imagine what they're thinking or feeling when they say something mean or hurtful. But if we don't try, then how will we ever grow as people?

When you're empathetic, you feel the feelings of others around you; you feel their happy thoughts as well as negative thoughts, and you can tell If they're lying or being honest with themselves. This can help relationships because it lets you know if someone's not telling the truth. But sometimes, we take empathy too far and start to believe everything that people say, even when it doesn't make sense. And then there's over-compassion, or "unchecked compassion," as the scientists call it. Unchecked compassion is when we feel bad for other people all the time, even if they don't deserve our sympathy, and this can be very harmful to them, even if they don't realize it's happening to them. Empathy isn't bad; it's just something that happens naturally to us and makes us better people overall. But sometimes it can get out of hand! So remember: empathy isn't always good for everyone around you; it depends on how much of it you have!

As humans, we're hard-wired to be empathetic. And sometimes it's easy for our empathy to take over and make us feel guilty for the things we want or do. So, it's also important to remember: that not everyone, or every situation, is worth your guilt! If you ever find yourself feeling bad about something you have done or said because another person wants you to feel bad about it, take a step back and ask yourself if this is worth it. Practice empathy and try to see things from their perspective, but if you genuinely feel you've done nothing wrong, and you've take the time to calmly explain your point of view, then don't let their pain become your burden. It is important for both parties to practice empathy; you shouldn't be the only one.

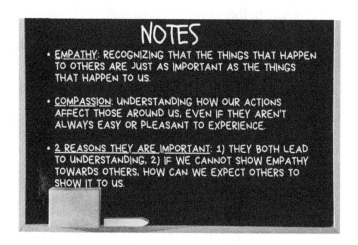

**NOTES**

- **EMPATHY**: RECOGNIZING THAT THE THINGS THAT HAPPEN TO OTHERS ARE JUST AS IMPORTANT AS THE THINGS THAT HAPPEN TO US.

- **COMPASSION**: UNDERSTANDING HOW OUR ACTIONS AFFECT THOSE AROUND US, EVEN IF THEY AREN'T ALWAYS EASY OR PLEASANT TO EXPERIENCE.

- **2 REASONS THEY ARE IMPORTANT**: 1) THEY BOTH LEAD TO UNDERSTANDING, 2) IF WE CANNOT SHOW EMPATHY TOWARDS OTHERS, HOW CAN WE EXPECT OTHERS TO SHOW IT TO US.

# Journal Prompts

1) Do you consider yourself an empathetic person? Why?

2) Do you tend to think about the perspective of others before making decisions?

3) Do you feel those closest to you show empathy towards you? Why?

4) If you answered 'no' to any of these questions, what do you think you can do to change this?

# STEP 4
## Accepting Change

Ever notice how it's easy to feel like you're going to fail when you're trying to make a change? Like, you know that thing you want to do is so important, but you're afraid that if you don't succeed at it this time, your life will be over? Well, I've good news for you: that's not true. I'm willing to bet that if you change something in your life, even something really small, you'll find yourself happier and more successful than ever. I used to be a lot like you, and I'm not just saying that because it helps me sound like I have experience. I was a teenager once, and I know what it's like to feel like time is flying and your whole life is passing by instantly. It's true: life changes fast. Changes happen, and they're part of life. That's not going to stop, and it's not bad. It's just the way things are! Change is a necessary and beautiful part of life. Our lives are an ever-changing landscape, and we must always look for new things to experience. Our brains constantly adapt to new inputs, so it's important to keep an open mind as we go through life. It's also important to be aware of our own biases and prejudices; we can't fully understand another person's experiences until we've put ourselves in their shoes.

I'm sure you've felt like this before: your emotions are up one day and down the next, or maybe you feel like nothing will ever get better for you. But here's the thing: it does get better. And even if it doesn't seem that way, trust me, you'll see. Things get harder, and then they get easier again; sometimes, you feel like you're spinning your wheels, and sometimes you feel like you're flying. You'll go through phases of feeling loved by the world and periods when you feel alienated from the people around you. And then there are those moments when it feels like nothing has changed, you still feel lonely or anxious or anxious about being alone, and those are the hardest ones to deal with. But here's what I want to tell you: Things in your life will never stop changing! It's part of being alive, which means that no matter how much we think our lives are going to stay the same, they will not stay that way for long. What matters is how we handle things in between those changes and how we respond when things don't go as planned or turn out differently than we expected them to.

You've got to remember that life is a series of changes, and not all of them are bad. Some of them are good! And some of them will make it hard for you to figure out what you want. But that's OK; you can get through it! You'll figure out where you fit in the world and your place, and everything will be fine. It's a fact of life: things shift. And sometimes, these shifts are hard. It's easy to get stuck in the past, but it's important to remember that change is a part of our lives, and we should learn how to deal with it when it happens. Here are some tips for managing your emotions when something changes: **Be honest with yourself:** If you're feeling like you're missing out on something because it's changing, that's OK! Try not to feel bad about your feelings or let them control you; you can still have fun and enjoy life despite whatever is happening around you. **Talk about it:** Talking about what's happening in your life is always good for keeping yourself grounded and focused on the present moment (which is all anyone can do!). You might even find someone else who has had similar experiences and talk about them together! And finally, **remember that you're not alone.** When we're upset or unhappy, it's easy to feel like everyone else around us lives a problem-free life. But don't forget that many other things are going on in their lives, too. We're all going through this together.

Why is change necessary for our lives anyway? You're probably already aware of the importance of change in your life. But what if I told you that every one of us has a lifelong need for it? That's right! We must be reminded daily how important change is to us and how much we can benefit from it. For example, one summer in college I wanted to go to a 3 month immersive language learning school to improve my Spanish. By the time summer arrived, I had not saved enough money to pay for the school, so instead, I signed up for a summer internship in Florida, at the last minute. I did not want to go to that summer internship. It was an unexpected, and very unwanted, change of plans. I was pretty sad about it. But, by the end of the summer I didn't want to leave Florida! I ended up making a ton of friends AND that internship was the reason I got a really good job in my field my senior year of college! So what's my point? My point is, I was genuinely crushed that I couldn't go to language school that summer, **but I did not allow those emotions to keep me down.** I let myself to fully feel my disappointment, but I did not criticize myself, nor my family, for not having enough money to pay for the school. I chose another route that summer, embraced the unknown, and ended up having an unexpectedly wonderful time. I also got a great career start from that internship. Change can be good if we go with it, rather than resist it.

The thing about change is that it's hard. It's easy to get comfortable with what you know and what you're used to, and it can be frustrating when something new comes along, and you have to adjust. But here's the thing: if you don't try, and if you don't make an effort to keep learning, then you could miss out on something great. So if you're feeling like things are getting stale for you in some way, or if it feels like there's not much space for new ideas in your life anymore, don't worry! There are always ways to improve things, no matter how much time has passed since your last big change. Sometimes it takes a lot of courage to make big changes, but sometimes it just takes a little courage! It's important to remember that change is good in life. It's the things that stay the same that we should be afraid of because change is a sign of growth. The world isn't always going to be like this. It's going to change, and sometimes those changes will be hard: new friends, new classes, new places. But they're also going to be exciting and fun! Think about how much better life would be if we all just accepted the positive aspects that come with change and went along with it.

We need change; we need to get up and do something new as often as possible! When we're stuck in a rut, we can get bored or even depressed. When we're bored or depressed, our brains stop working as well as they should be able to. This can lead to problems with our moods and ability to think clearly. But there are ways around this! You don't have to stay home all day if you don't want to. There are plenty of things out there that will keep you busy and ensure your brain is working as well as it can! Try something new every week or month; it'll feel good when you get going!

It's hard to believe that things can shift so quickly in a person's life. But they do, and it's best to be prepared for future potential changes. Knowing how to handle the emotions that can come with a change in your life is important. You don't want to get angry or upset when something happens because it will only make things worse. Instead, focus on what you can do now instead of what has happened. Things will get better! The unknown is difficult to think about. It's a part of life that can feel very scary. It can feel like your life is falling apart before your eyes! But experiencing change means you're growing and learning; growing both in your internal and external world. You might be feeling sad or nervous about moving away from home, making new friends, or whatever else it is that life changes bring up, but try not to let it get to you too much. Change always happens; there's no reason to let it take over your life if you can help it!

That said, I know this is a tricky subject, and I'm not going to pretend it's easy. But I think we can all agree that life is often frustrating. Things are always changing, and that change is often painful. But what if we could learn how to accept these changes? What if we could learn how to move through our pain quickly and efficiently? It's hard to accept that things are changing, and sometimes it's even harder to accept that they have changed outside our control. You just have to take things as they come and try not to overthink things too much! I used to be the person who always wanted what I didn't have. I wanted a boyfriend, but I didn't have one. I wanted a job in my field, but I had no idea what it would take to get one. I wanted my parents to appreciate me more, but they never did. But then, one day, things took a turn for the better. I decided I no longer wanted to be sad. Being sad all the time is exhausting! I chose to accept what I didn't have, I became grateful for what I had, and kept working towards my goals, knowing that if I never gave up, then one day, I would have the life I desired. And that was when I realized that maybe happiness wasn't about having what others had; it was about taking care of yourself and doing the best you could with what you had.

These experiences in my life lead me to this conclusion: There are some things you can't change.

You can never get back the time you lost or the people who were taken from you too soon. But what we CAN do is hold on to the good memories, give ourselves the grace to **feel** our emotions, learn from our experiences, and keep moving forward.

Unfortunately, a lot of people are afraid of change and this can stop them from moving forward in their lives. They're so focused on what they want and what they're not doing that they don't see the opportunity for improvement. But there are things you can do to make change easier on yourself: talk to someone who knows what they're doing when things change (like a friend), try taking a deep breath before reacting (like yoga), or just remember that this, too, shall pass. Life is a series of changes, and you will have to get used to many of them. You might be a teenager, but that doesn't mean you can't still learn new things about yourself and your world. You should always be asking questions! The more you know, the more comfortable you'll feel with yourself and the world around you. As with most things in life, change is something we have to accept in order to move forward. Change doesn't mean you have to like it, but it does mean that you need to learn how to deal with it.

If you want to make positive changes in your life then you need to accept them and move on from there.

Learning to accept change is an important step in living a fulfilling life. It doesn't matter how comfortable you are or how much you think you know, change happens in your life every day.

As for me, I don't let myself get stuck on the things that don't matter anymore. When I was younger, my whole identity was wrapped up in being "popular." But as I grew older and started seeing other people having the spotlight, I accepted that my phase of popularity has to go now. I have learned that sometimes it's OK not to have everything figured out before moving forward with something new. As long as you're making progress and improving yourself along the way, then there's no need for perfectionism! And having a purpose helps me keep going when things get tough or boring; it gives me something concrete about why I'm doing what I'm doing every day! Plus, it makes my life feel more meaningful.

In short, I know it can be hard to deal with change, but I promise it's worth it. When you learn to accept change and embrace the new, you'll find that life is so much easier. You'll find that things just work out better, even if they don't look like they should. Even if a new person comes into your life, or a new job comes along, or even if you have to move across the country, it's not all bad! You'll get through it because you're embracing change. You might not see this right away, but once you start letting things go, everything will be better for it! When we talk about change management, we're talking about a process that helps us get ready for the future by accepting what's happening now. The first step is to get clear on your goals. What are you trying to accomplish? How do you want things to be after this change? Once you've got those down, it's time to start thinking about how you're going to get there. That includes defining your end goal, as well as developing strategies for getting there (what kind of processes will be needed?). Finally, you must involve everyone involved in this process, so they feel like they're being heard and understood, which means giving them time and space for input into the solution. With time, I realized that if I could just get past my fear of change, I could be better prepared for whatever life threw my way. So instead of crying about it, I decided to tackle it head-on, and now? I love change. It's like an adventure every day! And you know what? The only way you can make sure you're ready for the adventure ahead is by learning how to embrace change when it comes your way.

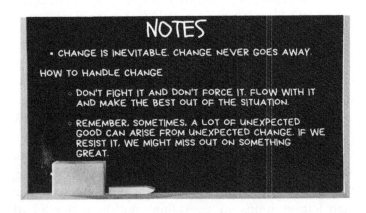

# Journal Prompts

1) How does change make you feel?  Do you find change difficult to accept?

2) Do you have any big goals for the next five years?  What are you doing to achieve those goals?  How will you feel if things don't go the way you expected?

3) Change is an inevitable part of life.  Does this fact make you feel anxious?  Do you think you can accept this fact?  Why?

# STEP 5
# Overcoming Criticism

There is a saying that goes, "If you want to be your own worst critic, you're going to be your own worst enemy." I think we can all relate. Sometimes we put ourselves down and feel like we aren't good enough. Sometimes we don't even realize how much of a perfectionist we are until someone else points it out. And sometimes, we just have some habits that make us feel less of ourselves than we are, like when we write more negative self-talk than positive self-talk. We are harsh and judgmental about ourselves.

Sometimes, we think that we're the only ones who feel this way. But it's not true. Everyone has a story like this. The difference is that we choose to believe that our story is "normal." We don't accept that there are other ways to feel or other ways to react when something goes wrong. We just want to be right all the time, so we can feel good about ourselves. But why do we do this? Why do we need to be right all the time? There are a million reasons why we're so harsh and judgmental about ourselves. I mean, it's easy to get caught up in the moment and say things like, "I'm not good enough," or "I'm ugly," or "I don't have any friends." But really, it's just a bunch of crap. We all have things that we feel we should be doing better, and we're right! We are all human, after all. But the truth is that no one is perfect, and there will never be one thing about us that will make us worthy of high praise or admiration from others. So stop being so hard on yourself! You'll end up with more friends, a more balanced life, and a much happier outlook on life if you can start treating yourself with kindness instead of harshness. It's hard to love yourself when you're constantly judging and being harsh on yourself.

Many of us can remember a moment when we were sitting around the dinner table, and one of our parents said something that made us feel bad about ourselves. It might have been something silly like "That shirt looks funny on you!" Or maybe they didn't say anything at all but just looked at us in an unfriendly way. The next day, we'd see our reflection in the mirror and think: "Wow, I'm really ugly today." Or maybe it wasn't your parents; maybe it was someone else who made us feel bad about ourselves. But what if there was a reason for this? And what if all these reasons were stacked up against each other, making us feel like we had no control over our lives? Sometimes, it's easy to fall into a cycle of self-criticism. You think something isn't good enough: your handwriting is too messy, your outfits are boring, your hair is too short (because all the popular girls at school have long hair). Maybe you even beat yourself up for not being perfect. This is all wrong. You're the only YOU who exists, and that's pretty awesome! You are a unique human being who deserves kindness and compassion, not criticism. Here are some ways that you can start treating yourself with more love and kindness today: Take a moment to remind yourself why you're doing something: "I'm reading this because I want to learn how to communicate better." Or "I'm wearing these jeans because they make me feel confident." Say something nice about yourself out loud (or write it down). For example: "You're smart!" or "You're pretty!" or "You're brave!" It will greatly improve your mood.

Judging yourself so harshly is a big part of what holds us back in life. We think we can't do something, or we think we're stupid. We've all done things that we regret later on. But we judge ourselves so harshly when these things happen because we feel like they make us look bad. And then when something does go wrong, we feel like an absolute failure and don't know how to fix it because nobody told us how to fix it! So don't be hard on yourself; just remember: there is no such thing as perfect. So stop blaming yourself for your faults and start loving yourself for being YOU!

There was also a time in my life when I had all this negativity around me that just seemed to keep me down. It was exhausting, and I knew it wasn't helping me get ahead at work or in my relationships. But then, one day, I decided to try something different: I tried to overcome my challenges through positive affirmations. Why not? After all, they'd worked for other people, like my best friend when she was going through a lot of hardships! And they seemed to help her feel more upbeat. She told me that she didn't have time for negative thinking because she had so much to accomplish instead of worrying about life. So why shouldn't I do the same thing? So that's what I did: every night before falling asleep, I would repeat these affirmations to myself over and over again until they were ingrained into my brain like a groove in a record. The first thing you need to do is to try and think of something that matters the most to you, at least once every day. You could even try writing it down if you like! After doing this for a few days, start thinking about what makes you truly happy, and then write down as many of those things as possible. You can also think about all the things that make you feel good and special. This process will help you think more positively because it will give you positive affirmations throughout your day! For example: "I am strong." "I can do anything." "I love myself." "I am loved." Those are just some examples of things that could help change how you feel about yourself! An affirmation that has helped me most is "I am capable of anything ". This affirmation helps me feel confident when I face challenges because it tells me that no matter what happens, I am capable of dealing with them. Another affirmation I use is "Every day is another opportunity to make a positive change in my life." This affirmation helps me focus on the positives in life and makes me realize how lucky we are to be here today, enjoying all these things around us, such as food, clothes, etc. "I have everything I need to succeed." This affirmation also helps me focus on the things that matter in life because once we get out of our comfort zone, then it becomes easy for us to commit to things in life that matter.

I think it's important to have a good self-image. But sometimes we can get so caught up in our own problems that we forget to appreciate the good things we already have in our lives. I believe that one reason why people hate themselves so much is that they don't feel good enough. They may feel like their parents never loved them, or their friends don't like them very much, or they don't have any skills or talents that other people have. But here's the thing: those thoughts are just going to make you feel worse. And that's not healthy for anyone—especially not for yourself. So here's what I need you to do: take a moment to think about how much better your life can be if you stop hating yourself. Think about all the things you've been able to accomplish because you love yourself and believe in yourself and are proud of who you are and what you stand for. Think of all the people who love and support you, whether they're family members, close friends, coworkers, teachers, clients, neighbors, or even random strangers who might recognize that self-love is really important! Imagine how much better their lives would be if they were able to give themselves some positive, loving attention too! If you want to believe that your story is worth telling and your future is worth creating and living…well then, this is only step one of your journey towards finding self-love!

By default, we want people to see us as more than our personality traits; we want them to see who we are as individuals. And if that's what we want from other people, why wouldn't it be nice if we could give ourselves that same gift? So go ahead: put down your mask and let yourself shine because self-love is the most important thing in the world. I know it sounds crazy, but I promise: it is.

My friend used to think that her self-worth depended on what other people thought of her. She used to think that if they thought she was smart or pretty or capable, then she was doing something right. But then one day, it hit her: none of those things are about being liked by other people. They're about making yourself happy and feeling good about who you are, inside and out: your personality and skill set, your goals and ambitions, everything that makes you an individual with your own thoughts and feelings and priorities, not just someone who wants approval from others because it makes them feel good about themselves too.

I'd like to tell you the well-known story of Ghyslain Raza, someone who rose from the ashes of cyberbullying and harassment when he was a 15 year old student, and is now a successful lawyer and thought provoker. During high school, he was teased and bullied by his classmates, and the whole world, because of his passion for the movies; he recorded himself mimicking a Star Wars character for one of his school projects and the video went viral. To escape being bullied, he dropped out of school and became depressed. But, over time, he overcame these harassments. Ghyslain Raza is a role model for anyone who has felt like they can never overcome deep depression. He rose above his teenage troubles, graduated from school, and became a successful lawyer. I've always felt his story was motivating because if he can overcome the nationwide criticism he endured as a teenager, we can overcome our problems, too. Let his journey of triumph motivate you and be a reminder that you do not have to accept less than what you deserve in life. Hurtful criticisms from others won't be the end of your story, if you don't allow them to be. **Be kind to yourself, especially when others are not.** Sometimes, your hardships will seem impossible to overcome; but with perseverance, self-love, and a positive mindset, you can defeat just about any problem.

When you start loving yourself and your life in a new way, it makes room for all sorts of amazing things: You'll find yourself getting closer to your friends and family in ways you never thought possible before. You'll have more energy because you'll have less stress about things outside of your control. And most importantly: your happiness will increase exponentially as a result!

Self-love is important because it allows us to see ourselves as we truly are. It gives us the space and courage to accept who we are and what we've done, without judgment or shame. It's also the basis for a fulfilling and healthy relationship with yourself, your body, and the world around you. Self-love is hard because it urges us to even accept and love our flaws, but that's okay! What isn't okay is when we don't feel confident in ourselves—which happens when we're in denial about our own strengths or abilities. The best way to start feeling more confident is by being kind to yourself and treating yourself with love and respect.

And don't forget about your relationships with other people! Try being mindful about how much time you spend with friends and family members so they feel like part of your support system too! It's easy to get caught up in day-to-day life, and it can be hard to remember that we're worth so much more than our jobs are or what we've done for other people. It's easy to forget how incredible we are, but I'm here to tell you that you're a force to be reckoned with. You have so much potential and power inside of you, and I am here to help you tap into that by practicing self-love. It's easy to forget when life gets busy, but when things get rough, remember that your worth doesn't depend on the money in your bank account or how many times you've been promoted at work—it's about who you are as a person.

I'm not saying it's easy. I know it's not easy to love yourself and accept yourself as you are. But I do believe that if we practice self-love in the right way, we can become better versions of ourselves and have the life we deserve. I've learned that one of the most important things I can do for myself is to stop putting myself down when others say or do things that are mean or hurtful. When someone says something mean to me, it doesn't make me feel bad about myself—it makes me feel bad about them. If someone says something mean to me, it means they don't understand me or who I am: their words don't represent how I want to be accepted by others. The second thing is accepting myself completely—both the good and bad parts of my personality. Sometimes we get so caught up in our faults that we forget all the good things about ourselves! That's why it's so important for us to remember everything about us that makes us unique—and also take care of ourselves so we can keep those things going strong over time! Finally, remember what you deserve in this life: happiness and joy! Don't settle for less than what you truly deserve.

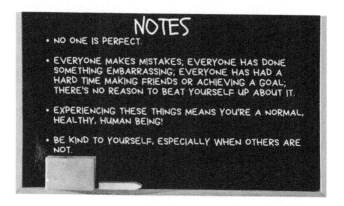

# Journal Prompts

1) When was the last time you were really critical of yourself? Do you feel you were being fair to yourself?

2) How do you react to criticism from others?

3) Do you criticize others often? If so, why?

4) Are you kind to yourself? If not, what are ways you can be more kind to yourself?

# STEP 6
# Setting Boundaries

When you're a teenager, it can be really hard to figure out what your boundaries are. You're just starting to understand what relationships mean and how they work, but there's a lot of pressure on you to socialize, exceed at school, and to look at the top of your game. It can feel like if you don't have any friends, you're missing out on some kind of social experience. But that's not necessarily true! You can have friends without being friends with everyone. What's important is that these friendships are healthy and positive for both parties involved. If you start hanging out with two new people and you notice they don't seem to respect your personal space or are pushy, you might keep hanging out with them just to have friends, or because they're popular and being friends with them could make you popular. But the fact is that this "friendship" won't be healthy for you in the long run. That's why it's so important for teens to learn how to set healthy boundaries in their relationships from an early age; this will help them develop healthy habits that will stick with them throughout their lives.

Boundaries are the metaphorical lines you draw around yourself and your belongings, and they're important because they help you feel completely safe in your own skin. When you have a boundary in place, it allows you to be free to explore without worrying about whether someone will walk up and try to take something from you. When I say "take something from you", it could be something physical like your favorite pen at school, or they could take your time, like having your lunch break wasted because your coworker wanted to talk the entire 30 minutes while all you wanted was to eat in silence. Once you know your boundaries, stick with them! You'll feel better about yourself when you know exactly how far away from your personal space you want others to be. This is something that we all need to be aware of, especially as we get older. It's important for us to maintain our personal boundaries because it allows us to feel like we have a sense of privacy in our lives. We can't control everything that happens around us and, sometimes, people will try to take advantage of this fact by asking us to do things that make us uncomfortable or push our limits. We need to learn how to protect ourselves from those who want something from us without asking permission first.

You need certain boundaries in order for your relationships with other people to be healthy. So, let's talk about the importance of our own personal safety! You see, when we share our time and space with others, we're putting ourselves at risk for harm, whether physical or emotional, so it's important that we have limits around how much time and space those people have access to us during those times.

If someone says something that makes you feel uncomfortable, or if you find yourself in a situation where you don't know how to say no to someone, then it's likely that your personal boundaries are being violated. **Personal boundaries are important for a variety of reasons:**

1) To protect yourself from harm and danger. If a friend tries to pressure you into doing something that makes you uncomfortable, then your personal boundary is being violated. You don't want to get hurt, so cut him/her out!

2) To ensure that you have time for yourself. If someone doesn't respect your personal boundaries (say, by not giving you enough space), then they're taking away something

important to make sure they can get their way with you. That's not cool!

3) To maintain integrity and authenticity in your relationships with others. When we stick to our own personal boundaries as much as possible, we help ourselves be more authentic both emotionally and physically.

Why is it hard for some people to set boundaries in their friendships and other relationships? It's a question that many of us have struggled with at one point or another. When we're young and our friends are mean, we think, "What did I do to deserve such treatment?" But then as we grow up, we realize that these friends weren't really mean on purpose, they just didn't know any better. You're learning how to stand up for yourself and say no, but when it comes to your friends, it's a little more difficult. How do you decide what boundary means? The truth is that boundaries are tricky to set in certain relationships. But when you don't set boundaries, you can find yourself in situations where you feel trapped, or at least not able to change your circumstances. Setting boundaries takes courage sometimes; you have to trust that people are going to respect your boundaries and be understanding, but if they don't respect your boundaries (because sometimes people will try and push past them anyway) you should not keep those kinds of people in your life.

I think that emotional boundaries are something that we all need to learn how to set. I remember the time I had a friend who was always trying to talk me into doing things that I really didn't want to do. She'd try to get me to go out for drinks with her, convince me to invite her to my apartment to hang out, or ask me things about my personal life that I didn't want to share. This went on for a while until finally one night when we were staying up late watching a show together and I was feeling tired and emotional from the day's events. My friend kept asking me if I wanted her to stay longer, but each time I said no because it wasn't what I needed right then. She got upset with me for not wanting her company, even though I spent time with her all afternoon. She didn't understand what it meant to respect my boundaries! Allowing someone else into your space isn't always what you want! It can be exhausting if they try too hard or insist too much on getting their way. I stuck by my decision and told her I was going to bed and I'd see her later. It was my first time standing up for myself with her and it felt good to stick to my boundary. I figured, if our friendship was ruined over this, then it wasn't a healthy friendship to begin with and I'd be okay with it ending. Luckily, that didn't happen! Eventually, we talked about it and she completely understood. In the moment, she felt offended, but she later agreed that it was a little irrational to be offended just because I needed some alone time after a hard day.

Implementing boundaries isn't always the easiest, but there are ways that you can try and get better at setting them without losing a person who cares about you. How do you know if a person is invading your emotional boundaries in the first place? Well, it's easy! If you feel anger, frustration, or disappointment when someone else doesn't respect the way that you have laid out your boundaries for them, then they are probably violating those boundaries. When a person violates your emotional boundaries, it can be hard to know how to respond. You may feel angry and frustrated with yourself for not being able to control what other people do. But there are ways to get back on track and learn from this experience. Remember that respecting others' emotions is just as important as respecting your own. If someone is taking advantage of your emotional boundary by treating you poorly or making you feel inferior in some way, then don't let them get away with it! But keep in mind that everyone has the right to their own emotions and that no one should be made to feel bad about them at any time.

I'm going to tell you about one of my favorite tricks for standing up for yourself when someone is treating me poorly. It's called "the white flag" technique which essentially means that you peacefully surrender instead of aggravating the fight. Here's how it works: when someone starts treating me like garbage, I get really quiet and just wait until they stop talking. Then I say something like "I feel like we're not communicating well enough," or "I don't know how else to say this." At this point, I will refuse to further engage in the discussion until we've both taken some time to think before we speak. For some people, this will make them even more angry and when this happens it's best to walk away and let them cool down. But, many times after using this technique, the person will choose to evaluate what they said and try to go about the conversation more calmly, or even try to make amends! It's a great way for both parties to stop and assess the situation, which will hopefully keep tempers from escalating!

Here are some other ways to set healthy boundaries:

1) Ask for what you need, and be open about how much of it you need. For example, if you need time alone, just say so. Or, let's say you and a friend are carpooling to work. If your friend doesn't want to

listen to loud music on the drive because he has a headache, he should say so in an assertive, but respectful, way, rather than huff and puff, and make other passive aggressive noises the entire drive.

2) Confidently speak your mind. If you're not comfortable with something, say so. Don't let your friends get away with doing things that make you uncomfortable, or even worse, make you feel like they don't care about your feelings at all. Say "no" when you mean "no," if other people are pushing you or are acting out of character. For example, if someone asks "can I borrow your car?", but their history of reckless driving and speeding tickets makes you uncomfortable lending your car to them, then just tell them no. It might be difficult for them not to get upset about this when they hear the answer, but it will be worth it for your peace of mind. And, once again, ask yourself; if someones gets angry at you, or no longer wants to be your friend, because of a boundary you respectfully set…do you really want them in your life?

3) Be direct. The easiest way to set healthy boundaries is by being clear and direct in what you want from a relationship. For example, if you're not comfortable

with someone bringing up the topic of politics or religion during a conversation, just let them know that's something that makes you uncomfortable. It doesn't have to be an issue for everyone else, it's just your preference not to get involved in such discussions!

4) Determine what you're willing to compromise on and what you're not.

Use your words to communicate your needs, wants, and limits. Be kind to yourself when setting boundaries—this will help you stay strong and clear-headed when it comes time for them to be tested! Keep in mind that sometimes it's okay to ask for what you want and other times it's better not to. Don't let others talk you into doing something you don't want to do or feel uncomfortable with. If someone asks you to do something, stand up for yourself and say no if it's not what you want to do for yourself or for them, even if it hurts their feelings. And most importantly, if someone makes a mistake, forgive them, but don't let them off the hook for repeating it again and again (or worse).

Let's say your best friend tells you that she needs to borrow $100 from you. You don't have it, so you tell her she can't have it. But then she comes back and says she needs it for groceries and gas, and if you don't give it to her now, she'll go without food or heat. What do you do? If you're like most people, the answer is probably "I'll give it to her." These are the consequences of not having boundaries: when you tell someone you can't do something, but they still insist on violating your boundaries and keep asking, you can develop hidden anger and resentment. It makes you feel powerless and helpless, and then you're also likely to start thinking about how things could be better if only you had more power to make your own decisions and to draw your boundaries. The result? More stress, more unhappiness, more stress...and on and on until we're all completely burned out!

This can be a difficult concept to grasp, but it's really not that complicated. When you don't set boundaries for yourself, you lose out on the opportunity to experience true freedom. You're not in control of your life and you don't get to decide what happens next. That's why it's so important to take a few minutes each day to think about what your boundaries are and how they might be affected by the things going on around you. It's a process that takes time and practice, but once you have those boundaries in place, they'll become second nature, and they'll help guide you through life with confidence and clarity.

One thing to note is that boundaries are flexible and can change throughout life. When you were younger, it made sense for you to follow your parents every word. If they put you on the local 5 year old soccer team, you just accepted it and tried to have fun. As a child, your greatest boundary with your parents might've been your adamant refusal to eat brussels sprouts! But as you get older and begin to learn more about yourself, your boundaries might shift. You might be a little more vocal if they try to force a particular sport or career path on you. If you were raised by parents who were not very supportive of your individual goals and dreams, but who still love you and want the best for you, it might've been helpful for them to know that they shouldn't try to persuade you into, say, becoming a doctor when you clearly want to be an artist. Your goals and dreams are just as important as their desires for you. You may have decided to bow down under the pressure believing that this is just "how it is with parents", but at the end of the day, your parents can only guide you. Ultimately, your life's path is up to you. You should try to tell them in a loving way that this is something that you're passionate about and following someone else's dreams will crumple up your own sense of individuality, and ask them to guide you in all phases of your life but, now that you're getting older, they should respect you when it comes time for your own decision-making process.

In short, healthy boundaries are important in our lives because they allow us to have a sense of security and control, which is crucial for the way we feel about ourselves. You can't control what other people are going to do, but you can control what you will tolerate and what you will not. Having healthy boundaries means that you're able to say no when someone asks you to do something that makes you feel uncomfortable or unsafe. It also means that you're able to say yes when someone asks you to do something that makes you feel good! When we feel like we don't have control over what happens in our lives, it can be very hard for us to feel confident and self-assured. We may even develop feelings of depression and anxiety as a result. But when we have healthy boundaries and know how they work, it becomes easier for us to be strong in those moments where we need them most!

# NOTES

- BOUNDARIES ARE THE METAPHORICAL LINES YOU DRAW AROUND YOURSELF AND YOUR BELONGINGS.

- THEY HELP MAINTAIN INTEGRITY AND AUTHENTICITY IN OUR RELATIONSHIPS.

- THEY ARE FLEXIBLE AND CAN CHANGE THROUGHOUT LIFE.

- BOUNDARIES ALLOW US TO HAVE A SENSE OF SECURITY AND CONTROL.

## Ways to Set Boundaries

- ASK FOR WHAT YOU NEED.
- CONFIDENTLY SPEAK YOUR MIND.
- BE DIRECT.
- DETERMINE WHAT YOU'RE WILLING TO COMPROMISE ON AND WHAT YOU'RE NOT.

You can't control what other people are going to do, but you can control what you will tolerate.

# Journal Prompts

1) Do you set boundaries? What would you say is the hardest thing about setting healthy boundaries?

2) Have you ever felt one of your boundaries was crossed? Explain what happened.

3) How do you feel when people don't respect your boundaries?

4) List at least 2 new boundaries you plan to implement in your life and write why you need these boundaries. Practice saying them aloud.

# STEP 7
# Self Care

I've always been a big believer in the importance of self-care and self-love. I think it's important to treat yourself with care and to make sure that you're taking time out for yourself, whether it's having a massage or going on a long walk by yourself. It's also important to be kind to your body, and give it what it needs in order to function at its best. I'm sure you know that when you're young, it can be hard to care about yourself. You're just trying to find your way in this big world, and you feel like you're always being pulled in different directions by people and situations. You don't have the time to take care of yourself and just relax, you have to be on top of your game all the time. But what happens if you don't take care of yourself? What happens when the stress gets too much for you? What kind of person are YOU going to be then? A good friend told me once that she thought her best self was when she was doing things for herself, when she took time for herself, and didn't try so hard at everything else. That's an important lesson: we've got to learn how to prioritize ourselves sometimes because we're only human! So, remember to do things that make you feel good about yourself (like reading a book about self-love), go for walks with friends who make you smile, or volunteer at an animal shelter! You should also remember to take care of your body; you have to make sure you eat right, get plenty of sleep, and exercise regularly. You should also make sure that your mental health is in check by meditating or practicing yoga regularly, for example.

Self-care is a valuable thing. It's what keeps you healthy, happy, and sane. But it's not just for the big stuff like whether or not you're going to change your career because you're not passionate about it. It can also be applied to the small stuff, like how your skin feels after a hard day at school, or how your hair looks when you tried that new hair product. Whether you're doing it for yourself or for someone else, self-care is something everyone should try to incorporate more often in their lives. When you take care of yourself, it shows that you care about your own well-being and the well-being of others around you. And when people see that kind of dedication in someone else... Well, let's just say they tend to want to do the same for themselves!

Frankly, self-care is something that many of us take for granted, but it is actually one of the most important things we can do for ourselves. It's an act of kindness to ourselves that allows us to be the best versions of ourselves and avoid burnout, fatigue, stress, and anxiety. When we're not taking care of ourselves, we're not giving our best selves to our family or our friends. We're also missing out on key opportunities for personal growth and improvement. Self-care doesn't have to be complicated or time-consuming, it just needs to be something you do every day so that you can feel amazing and at peace with yourself on the inside and out! It's not just a luxury, it's a necessity. Here are some benefits of self-care:

1) You will feel better physically and mentally.

2) You will have more energy, which means you can do more things!

3) You will be less stressed out, and stress has been shown to cause diseases like cancer and heart disease as well as depression and anxiety (which can cause you to make poor decisions).

4) You might even find that you sleep better or feel more rested when you do take care of yourself!

Now, let's go over various forms of self-care and how you can implement those practices in your life: I've always been a fan of sleeping, but I'd never really considered it to be a form of self-care. That is, until I got sick. I knew that sleep was important to my health, as anyone who has ever been sick will tell you, but I had never thought of it as something that would make me feel better emotionally or spiritually. Until one night after a long day at work, when I was lying in bed and realized how much more clear-headed I felt after getting 7 to 8 hours of proper sleep. So now when things get tough or stressful, I try to take an hour or two before bed every night and just relax. It's helped me cope with so many situations in my life and has kept me on track. That's why sleep is one of the most important things you can do to support your emotional health. It's not just a matter of getting enough sleep, it's an investment in yourself. When you're well-rested and feeling good, you're more likely to make healthy decisions, like eating right and exercising regularly. And those healthy choices will help support your emotional health in many ways, including helping you feel more optimistic and less stressed out.

You may have heard that sleep helps our brains grow new cells and keep them healthy, but did you know it can also help us manage stress? Sleep is important for keeping our moods steady, which means we'll be more likely to feel like ourselves and do well at work or school. It also helps us deal with the challenges in our lives without feeling overwhelmed by them. Plus, if you don't get enough sleep then your body may start to produce less cortisol, the hormone that helps regulate blood sugar levels and keeps us calm, which means that it can be harder for us to manage stress effectively! If you don't sleep enough, it can lead to problems with concentration in school and work. Research shows that lack of sleep also makes it harder for you to focus on tasks that require attention. It's also important to make sure you get enough sleep because studies have found that people who don't get enough sleep are more likely than others to develop depression or anxiety disorders later in life. Sleep allows us to recover from physical and mental stress and helps us to maintain our mental health, body temperature, and immune system. Sleeping also helps our body repair damaged cells and tissues, which is essential for the prevention of many diseases. For instance, over a long period of time, lack of sleep can lead to obesity and diabetes, which are both linked to heart disease.

You may have also heard that exercise is good for your health, but did you know it can also be a form of self-care? It's true! When you exercise regularly, you're doing something nice for yourself. You're showing yourself some love by taking care of your body and giving it what it needs to function at its best. And it's not just about the physical benefits: regular exercise helps keep your mind sharp and active too! By engaging in physical activity, you'll get a chance to break free from the stresses of everyday life and let yourself relax just a little bit. It's a form of self-care and self-love because it helps us take care of ourselves. We tend to neglect ourselves when we're busy, we miss the things we need and want, and when we finally have time to check in with ourselves, we're usually exhausted and stressed out. But when we exercise regularly, it gives us a chance to sit down with ourselves and make sure we're eating well, getting enough sleep, and taking care of our bodies well. It's also a chance to let go of some stress from the day as it's a way to enjoy our bodies in a way that doesn't involve scrolling through social media or other distractions. Regular exercise helps you feel more like yourself. When you're exercising regularly, you can see yourself grow stronger physically and emotionally as well, you can see yourself become more capable of doing things that used to seem impossible or unreachable (like running a marathon or finishing that project at school), or just feeling like you can face anything head-on.

But did you know that there's also a correlation between eating healthily and feeling loved? I was always a healthy eater. I loved fruits and vegetables, and I thought that eating fast food was a waste of money. But when I got into my twenties, everything changed. I started eating more processed foods, more sugar, and more alcohol. And suddenly, I felt like I had no energy to do anything but lay around on the couch all day. It was terrible! According to my doctor, I needed to change my diet, and fast. So I started eating more fruits and vegetables, less sugar, and processed foods (which are usually full of salt), as well as exercising regularly at the gym every day. And it worked! My energy levels went back up and my mood stabilized. It's important to me now that other people know that healthy eating isn't just about being healthy; it's also about being happy! I'm not saying that if you don't eat healthily your body will fall apart; what I am saying is that if your body is given the right nutrients, then it can perform at an optimal level. And when you feel good about how you look and how you feel inside, then you're much more likely to feel happy and confident in your life.

Social media can be deemed as another example: It can be a great way to keep in touch with friends and family. But if you use it too much, it can have negative effects on your mental health. People who spend too much time on social media are more likely to suffer from insomnia and depression. The same goes for people who constantly check their phones. These people may experience headaches and other physical symptoms when they're not using their phones. They may feel anxious about missing out on something or feel overwhelmed by all the information they're receiving from other people's posts and comments. They may also begin to feel disconnected from the real world around them because they spend so much time looking at screens rather than interacting with others face-to-face (which helps us form relationships). Finally, there's the financial side of things: If you're spending a lot of time on social media and mindlessly scrolling through the viral trends and posts, then you could end up losing money because you're always buying the latest viral gadget, or the newest clothing item some celebrity promoted, just because everyone you follow on social media has these things. Most of the time, these trends decline quickly, and then you're out of money and stuck with something you probably didn't really want in the first place.

So, if you're someone who tends to feel lonely or isolated on the internet, it might be time to take a break from social media for a while and focus on getting some face time with real people in your life. Or maybe you just need some rest from the stress of being on social media all day long, so take an hour out of your day and get off the grid! Taking your time off social media is not just about turning off your phone or laptop; those are great ways to disconnect, but they are not guaranteed to remove your stressors unless you make use of your free time in a productive way. It's about taking time out of your day for yourself, to do something that doesn't involve checking your phone or watching TV. And guess what? You can do this without feeling guilty! It doesn't have to be hard or complicated. Here are some suggestions:

1) Go outside for a walk or run (even if it's just around the block)

2) Do some yoga or meditation.

3) Get lunch with a friend or family member.

4) Take a hot bath with candles lit.

5) Make an appointment with your favorite salon (you'll feel amazing afterward!)

Rushing towards the imaginary world of social media because of FOMO (the fear of missing out) is real. It can be paralyzing, and it can keep you from doing the things that are most important to you. But it doesn't have to be this way! When we're afraid of missing out on something good, it's because we think we don't deserve that opportunity. But here's the thing:

you don't have to miss out on your big moments because of these fears. You don't have to miss out on your big moments because they're fleeting; you can catch them even without the help of social media, because taking a short break from constant usage of social media can be a great way of getting in touch with the real world and dissolving your fear of missing out!

Getting in touch with support groups is also a phenomenal way of practicing self-care. It's common to feel frustrated, nervous, or overwhelmed by the emotional challenges you face. You might feel like you're alone in your struggle; you might also feel like no one can understand what you're going through. That's where support groups come in handy! They offer a safe space for people to share their stories, ask questions, and receive support from others just like them. The benefits of support groups for our emotional health are endless: they help us process and work through issues that affect us personally; they allow us to make friends who understand what we're going through; they help us deal with stress; and so much more! One of the most important benefits of support groups for our emotional health is that they allow us to talk about things that we might not be able to talk about with anyone else. We can express our feelings and share our experiences with other people who have gone through similar experiences. Another benefit of support groups is that they help us learn new coping mechanisms and develop new ways of thinking that can help us deal with difficult situations in the future. We learn how other people have handled similar situations, which helps us understand what might work best for us. They're an amazing way to let your feelings out and learn how to manage them. When you're in one of these groups, you don't have to worry about whether or not you'll be judged, you just get to talk about whatever's on your mind!

Support groups are a great place to get emotional health help. They can be found in many different places, from churches to yoga studios to workplaces. They are an important part of our mental health and well-being, and it's important that you take advantage of them. First off, don't worry; you're not alone. According to the American Psychological Association (APA), over 1 in 3 adults suffer from a mental disorder at some point in their lives. And while there's no cure-all or one-size-fits-all method for dealing with these issues, there are other people out there who've been there before, and are willing to comfort you. But what can you do if you're having trouble finding support groups for your emotional health? A lot of people turn to online forums like Reddit and Quora, but don't be afraid to reach out and ask for help! There's no better way to do this than by simply asking someone, whether that person is a friend, family member, or fellow sufferer of the same struggles as yourself. You never know where their experience could take you, but there's always hope!

And finally, here are a few more tips with fun and simple ways to boost your emotional health (and your mood) when you're feeling down:

1) Go for a walk in nature! Try going to a park or even just taking a stroll in your neighborhood. If you're able to get outside for more than just a quick run-in, observe the bounties of nature, try getting some fresh air, and take a deep breath of clean air. It'll make you feel better and it might even give you the boost you need to tackle the rest of your day.

2) Take a bubble bath! When we think about taking baths, we probably think about relaxing and unwinding after a long day. A nice bath can actually help clear your head and give you some relief from stress. So if it's been a while since you've genuinely had time for one (or maybe never), try giving yourself an extra long soak today!

3) Play with your dog or cat, or even just walk around the house with those furry little creatures!

4) Relax on the couch with a good book and a cup of tea.

5) Take a nap! A quick 20 -30 minute nap is a wonderful way to rejuvenate yourself halfway through a rough day. If you don't feel sleepy, try laying down and closing your eyes for a few minutes. It's very relaxing and you never know how much you needed this break until you do it. Your body will thank you.

6) Although it is preferred that you find an activity that does not involve your phone, I am going to include this option: playing a quick game You can play games to keep yourself engaged. The best kind of games to improve your mental health and emotions are those that can be played anywhere, at any time. Games like Candy Crush Saga, Clash of Clans, and Animal Crossing are perfect for this. You can play these games whenever you get a chance, whether it's in the morning before school, on your lunch break, or on your way home. The great thing about these games is that they don't require much effort from the player. They're very easy to pick up and play, which is why they make great distractions from other activities. Another reason why these kinds of games are great for improving your mental

health and emotions is that they're social in nature. You have to interact with other players if you want to advance through the levels, or even just try to win a match against another player. This type of interaction helps keep your mind active and engaged with other people while also helping you feel more positive emotions like happiness or excitement.

As teenagers, we are often at the mercy of our emotions. When we're having a bad day, it's easy to forget that there are many ways to make that feeling go away. So always remember to make time for yourself. It's easy to get caught up in the craziness of being a teenager and neglecting ourselves. If someone is telling you what to do or how to feel without any regard to your personal desires and wishes, they might not understand what it's like to be a teenager and their advice might not be very helpful! They might not even know what they're talking about; maybe they've never experienced being in your position themselves. So learn to trust yourself, listen carefully, and make your own decisions based on what feels right for YOU (as long as it's safe, of course)! The truth is, nobody's perfect, not even you! So practice self-compassion when you need it. When something goes wrong in your life, sometimes it's hard to feel good about yourself because you feel like you deserve this. If this happens often enough, though, it can start to affect your self-esteem and make it harder for you to see yourself as worthy of happiness or success. So try reframing these failures as learning opportunities! The more you learn from them and improve yourself as a result, the better off everyone will be in the long run.

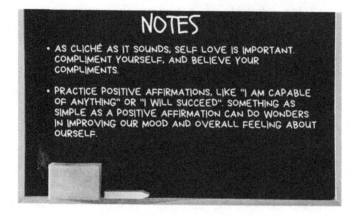

**NOTES**

- AS CLICHÉ AS IT SOUNDS, SELF LOVE IS IMPORTANT. COMPLIMENT YOURSELF, AND BELIEVE YOUR COMPLIMENTS.

- PRACTICE POSITIVE AFFIRMATIONS, LIKE "I AM CAPABLE OF ANYTHING" OR "I WILL SUCCEED". SOMETHING AS SIMPLE AS A POSITIVE AFFIRMATION CAN DO WONDERS IN IMPROVING OUR MOOD AND OVERALL FEELING ABOUT OURSELF.

# Journal Prompts

1) How often do you take time for yourself?

2) Do you ever feel like you don't have enough time to do things that make you happy?

3) What are your favorite ways of taking care of yourself?

4) How can you consistently implement at least 1 of the self care practices you listed into your life?

5) Do it! Do the self care practice!  It can be something you do once a day, once a week, or once a month; just make sure you do something for yourself, **consistently**!

# STEP 8
# Practice!!

Let's summarize the lessons from all the steps mentioned in this book:

1) We are all emotional, and it's important to understand what causes us to feel a certain way. If you're not sure why you're upset, take a step back and think about what happened and why.

2) If you find yourself getting triggered by things like stress (which can happen at any time), try spending more time doing activities that you enjoy and less time on things that make you stressed out or anxious.

3) People are not always right, but they are usually trying their best to get through their day in a manner that works for them. Take some time to really listen to another person's perspective on

any issue and see if they have anything valid or valuable to add to it. Ask yourself: What am I missing here? Why can't this person see things my way? How will this impact me?

4) It's important, not only as a teenager but also as an adult, that you accept change as an inevitable part of your life without getting angry or upset by it, because it's going to happen whether you want it or not.

5) The inner critic is a negative voice that can make you feel bad about yourself. It's what you think about yourself when you're not in the mood for being kind to yourself. It's the voice that says things like "I'm not good enough," "I'm a loser," or "I'll never be able to do it." The way I see it, the inner critic is just another part of your brain trying to protect you from pain and hurt. But there's no reason why YOU have to listen to it! You can practice self-compassion while also ignoring the negative thoughts that come up when you're feeling down.

6) Setting boundaries is one of the most important things you can do to manage your emotions. It's not always easy, but it's crucial to your long-term well-being. If someone says or does

something that upsets you, try to stay calm and explain what they did or said that upset you. If they don't change their behavior, let them know that their behavior is unacceptable and that you need it to stop. It's also important to communicate with people who make you angry in a way that doesn't make them feel attacked or like they've done something wrong.

7) Once you've acknowledged your emotions and set your boundaries, the next step is to engage in some self-care. Self-care is exactly what it sounds like—taking care of yourself through activities such as meditation, exercise or journaling can help put things into perspective for you and allow you to focus on what matters most (like your relationship with your family and friends). It also gives you time to reflect on how you're feeling so that when an emotion arises again later on (like when an issue arises at home), it won't overwhelm or overwhelm others around you.

And that's it! The last step is to practice! You've learned how to manage your emotions and think more clearly, and now it's time to go out into the world and use those skills! There are going to be times when you don't handle a situation perfectly, but that's okay, it happens. The important thing is that you didn't give up, and that you stayed true to yourself. I know it can be hard not to get discouraged, but try not to let it get in your way! Remember: these habits take practice, so keep using them until they become natural for you.

In the past year, I've learned a lot about managing my emotions. I used to be really reactive, and I'd get really mad at things that happened in my life without even thinking about them. But now, I tend to take a step back and reflect on what happened before reacting. That's helped me stay calm under pressure and prevented me from being taken advantage of by others. So, don't let yourself get too caught up in the moment. Think about the bigger picture before you react, and think about why you're reacting in the first place. Don't make assumptions about people's intentions or motivations when something happens. If someone does something hurtful or inappropriate, don't assume they're trying to be mean; instead, ask them why they did it and see if there's any way for both of you to move on together. Have a routine that includes activities that make you feel good. If you can find something that makes you feel good every day, then it will help you manage your emotions.

Another thing that has helped me manage my emotions is by learning how to recognize what exactly is going on inside me when I'm feeling angry or sad or anxious. By learning how to pay attention and listen for what's happening in my body, especially if there's an emotion coming up for me (like sadness), then I can figure out what needs attention before it gets out of control and turns into something bigger than itself. And this helps me get back in control of myself, so I'm not stuck with any negative feelings anymore!

It might feel difficult to practice emotional management and maturity if you are surrounded by emotionally immature people. You can't always control the emotions of others, but you can definitely take steps to manage your own. When you're around emotionally immature people, it's easy to get caught up in their drama and become overwhelmed. You might feel like you're the only sane person in the room and wonder how you're supposed to handle all your emotional baggage. So how can you manage their and your emotions when you're surrounded by such people? Stay calm! It's important that everyone else feels safe around you, so there's no need for them to feel threatened by your intensity or your ability to stay calm under pressure. For example, if you're getting upset and you want to yell at the person next to you, ask yourself why. Why are they making me so mad? What is it about them that makes me want to yell at them? If you can't figure out why they're making you angry, ask yourself what your reaction would be if the situation had been reversed. Would it be okay for them to treat you like that? If not, how do you make sure that if someone treats you this way again, it doesn't hurt your feelings or make you feel bad? The more aware of your emotions and how they affect others that we are, the better able we are to deal with them effectively.

Additionally, don't try too hard. If someone does something stupid or says something hurtful, try not to take it personally. If they don't know better, then it isn't really their fault; it's just a sign of immaturity! Make sure you know how to take care of yourself first. Sometimes we get so caught up in other people's emotions that we forget how our own feelings can affect us. Taking a few minutes to yourself each day will help you stay relaxed and energized throughout the day. Don't take on other people's emotions! It's easy to get caught up in someone else's drama, but if you do, it can cause problems for everyone involved, including yourself! You don't want to be known as "the one who doesn't understand." And remember that everyone has a different set of skills and abilities. Some people might not be able to handle certain situations very well yet (or at all), so keep this in mind when talking about things with emotionally immature people, they may not understand what you mean or why you feel this way.

After all, they're supposed to get over their hurt feelings and move on. But they can't. They just can't! And it's not your fault. You're trying your best to help them process their emotions in healthy ways, but they just keep going back to the same place over and over again. So don't take things personally: When someone is acting immaturely around you, it's important not to take it personally. Instead of thinking something like "Why did they do that? Do they hate me?" think more like "They're acting out of pain." Be kind and understanding with everyone around you, even if they aren't behaving well at the moment. Sometimes people are just having a hard time processing things, and that doesn't mean they are being intentionally rude or unkind toward others; it just means that their brain and heart aren't working very well as a team right now.

So, it's important to remember that it's normal to experience mood swings and emotional outbursts. You should know that it is perfectly fine to ask for help when you need it. When you feel upset and emotional, take some time to think about what led up to the feeling. If possible, talk with someone who cares about you and can help calm you down. It can also help if you write down what happened in order to keep track of your thoughts and feelings so that they don't get lost in the moment.

I hope this book has helped you better understand how to manage your emotions. If you ever feel like you just can't deal with everything going on, or think that your emotions are out of control, come back and reference it. We hope you find comfort in knowing that many other youngsters your age have also struggled with their emotions. I know that regulating your emotions can be hard, and I want to remind you that you can get the help you need to feel as supported as possible. After you've read the book, ask your friends to read it so they can also get the help they need in order to manage their emotions. I would also suggest that you talk to your parents about the things that are mentioned in this book, so they can better understand how to help you manage your emotions. They may not have an answer for you right away, but they'll be able to help you manage the challenges that come with this kind of situation.

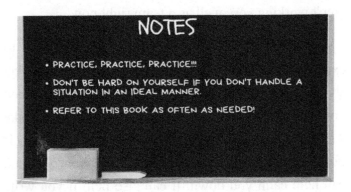

**NOTES**

- PRACTICE, PRACTICE, PRACTICE!!!
- DON'T BE HARD ON YOURSELF IF YOU DON'T HANDLE A SITUATION IN AN IDEAL MANNER.
- REFER TO THIS BOOK AS OFTEN AS NEEDED!

# Journal Prompts

1) What is the most important thing you learned from this book?

2) Can you visualize yourself practicing the methodologies written in this book in your day-to-day life?

3) How did your emotions or perspective change after reading this book?

4) Do you feel more confident in your ability to manage your emotions in a more healthy way? If not, why? Don't forget to refer to this book as often as needed!

Made in the USA
Monee, IL
05 October 2023